The Syntax and Semantics of the Nominal Construction

Potsdam Linguistic Investigations
Potsdamer Linguistische Untersuchungen
Recherches Linguistiques à Potsdam

Edited by/Herausgegeben von/Edité par

Peter Kosta, Gerda Haßler, Teodora Radeva-Bork,
Lilia Schürcks and/und/et Nadine Thielemann

Vol./Bd. 8

Frankfurt am Main · Berlin · Bern · Bruxelles · New York · Oxford · Wien

Diego Gabriel Krivochen

THE SYNTAX AND SEMANTICS OF THE NOMINAL CONSTRUCTION

A Radically Minimalist Perspective

PETER LANG
Internationaler Verlag der Wissenschaften

Bibliographic Information published by the Deutsche Nationalbibliothek
The Deutsche Nationalbibliothek lists this publication in the Deutsche Nationalbibliografie; detailed bibliographic data is available in the internet at http://dnb.d-nb.de.

Cover Design:
Olaf Gloeckler, Atelier Platen, Friedberg

ISSN 1862-524X
ISBN 978-3-631-62448-7
© Peter Lang GmbH
Internationaler Verlag der Wissenschaften
Frankfurt am Main 2012
All rights reserved.

All parts of this publication are protected by copyright. Any utilisation outside the strict limits of the copyright law, without the permission of the publisher, is forbidden and liable to prosecution. This applies in particular to reproductions, translations, microfilming, and storage and processing in electronic retrieval systems.

www.peterlang.de

Editorial

The series *Potsdam Linguistic Investigations – Potsdamer linguistische Untersuchungen – Recherches linguistiques à Potsdam* presents cutting-edge fundamental linguistics research carried out at the University of Potsdam. Its major goal is to publish collection of articles, conference proceedings and monographs on contemporary issues in the fields of Slavic languages and literature, Romance studies, English and American studies, German studies and general linguistics. A special focus of study is the formal, functional and cognitive description of language. The following areas of linguistics will seek to develop their own profile: phonology, morphology, syntax (with special attention to generative syntax), semantics, pragmatics (discourse analysis, speech act theory), sociolinguistics and language contact.

We do not set any theoretical, methodological or geographical boundaries. The series will serve greatly as a forum for young scholars as well as other researchers working in various linguistic fields and frameworks in Potsdam or elsewhere. The indication of Potsdam stands for the crucial importance and outstanding quality of linguistics research at the University of Potsdam. On the other hand, researchers from other Universities with proven excellence of their work are most welcome to publish their doctoral dissertations, habilitation monographs or conference proceedings in this series. The languages of publication are German, English and French.

Editorial

Die Reihe *Potsdam Linguistic Investigations – Potsdamer linguistische Untersuchungen – Recherches linguistiques à Potsdam* ist eine Plattform für linguistische Forschungen an der Universität Potsdam. Sie publiziert Sammelbände und Monographien zu aktuellen Fragen der zeitgenössischen internationalen Linguistik aus den Disziplinen Slavistik, Romanistik, Anglistik/Amerikanistik, Germanistik und Allgemeine Linguistik. Ein besonderer Schwerpunkt liegt in der formalen, funktionalen und kognitiven Sprachbeschreibung. Darin bilden vor allem die Bereiche Phonologie, Morphologie, Syntax (unter besonderer Berücksichtigung der generativen Syntax), Semantik, Pragmatik (Diskursanalyse, Sprechhandlungstheorie, Geschlechterforschung), Soziolinguistik und Sprachkontakt ihre eigenen Profile.

Wir wollen keine theoretischen, methodischen oder lokalen Grenzen setzen. Deshalb richtet sich die Reihe sowohl an Nachwuchswissenschaftler als auch an Kollegen in Potsdam und außerhalb Potsdams, die in verschiedenen Richtungen, Modellen und theoretischen Ansätzen der modernen Linguistik arbeiten. Der Hinweis auf den Standort Potsdam soll zum einen die herausragende Bedeutung der linguistischen Forschung an dieser Universität signalisieren. Andererseits bedeutet die Nennung nicht, dass ausschließlich Forschungsergebnisse (einschließlich Dissertationen, Habilitationen und Konferenzsammelbände) veröffentlicht werden, die von Linguistinnen und Linguisten an der Universität Potsdam stammen. Die drei Publikationssprachen sind Deutsch, Englisch und Französisch.

Editorial

La serie « *Potsdam Linguistic Investigations – Potsdamer linguistische Untersuchungen – Recherches linguistiques à Potsdam* » représente une plate-forme d'études linguistiques à l'université de Potsdam. Elle publie des recueils et des monographies sur les questions actuelles de la linguistique contemporaine internationale dans les domaines des études des langues slaves et romanes, anglaise et américaine, des langues germaniques et de la linguistique générale. Un point principal de recherche est posé sur la description formelle, fonctionnelle et cognitive des ces langues. Dans ces domaines, on met l'accent sur les profils de la phonologie, morphologie, syntaxe (en tenant compte de la syntaxe générative), sémantique, pragmatique (l'analyse du discours, la théorie des actes de la parole, la recherche sur le genre), la sociolinguistique où la linguistique de contact.

Nous ne voulons pas poser des limites dans la théorie, la méthode et le lieu de recherche. C'est pourquoi la série invite les jeunes chercheurs ainsi que les collègues de Potsdam et des autres universités qui travaillent dans les secteurs de la linguistique moderne. Le titre de la série veut démontrer d'un coté l'excellente qualité de la recherche linguistique à Potsdam sans toutefois exclure les autres. Cela veut dire que nous acceptons et nous invitons les linguistes de Potsdam et de l'extérieur (inclus les thèses de doctorat et d'habilitation et les actes de colloques). Les trois langues de publication sont : l'allemand, l'anglais et le français.

Acknowledgements

I would like to thank those who have been of crucial importance either for the content of the present work or for creating the optimal atmosphere in which the research could be best conducted. My deepest gratitude to Dr. Manuel Leonetti, without whom this monograph could have never been finished (or even started). The invaluable conversations and communications with him have undoubtedly improved both this particular work and my competence as a researcher. He has proven a great man as well as a brilliant linguist in countless occasions. When I have not followed his suggestions, it is the monograph that has suffered. Equal thanks go to Mg. Cristina Spínola, who has always been there kindly supporting my work even when the situation was not the best imaginable. I hope both her personal and professional support are appropriately acknowledged. They have both taken their chances with me and I sincerely hope not to have disappointed them. Dr. Michael T. Putnam (Mike) and Dr. Katarzyna Miechowicz-Mathiasen (Kasia) have also been of great importance for both the monograph and me. Their friendship and knowledge are very valuable for me, and have hopefully made me a better linguist and a better person, and I am grateful for having met such extraordinary people during this quest.

A proper acknowledgment of Dr. Peter Kosta's contribution to my career would deserve a whole chapter. May it suffice to say that I have greatly benefited from his friendship and knowledge, and he has given me the opportunity to "spread the word" about Radical Minimalism in conferences and seminars. We both know I will not be able to pay him back, I just hope I can live with that on my conscience.

Last, but most importantly, I would like to thank my father, Sergio, who supports my career and has made great efforts to give me the possibility to go to Germany and work in Potsdam University; my sister Natalia, for being always there when I needed some distraction and fun, and also a kind word, and for knowing so much about music; and very specially my wife, Roxana. Without her, my life would undoubtedly be poorer, and I feel very privileged to have her by my side, supporting me and listening to endless hours of syntactic talk. I owe her more than phonological matrix availability allows me to Spell-Out.

Finally, I would like to dedicate this monograph to my grandfather, Dr. Med. Alfredo Caba, the kindest man I have ever met, a model of honor and rectitude, and like a father to me. May this work be my humble homage to him.

Contents

Foreword 11

Chapter 1: An Introduction to Radical Minimalism 13
0   Introduction 13
1   Radical Minimalism and the Natural World 13
1.1   Radical Minimalism as a model for Quantum Linguistics 16
1.2   Generation in Radical Minimalism: Merge revisited 22
2   The Architecture of the System: OT, MP and RM 30
2.1   Dynamic Workspace 31
2.2   GEN = Generator 31
2.2.1 Against "Self Merge" 32
2.2.2 Against unrestricted distinct Merge 34
2.3   EVAL = Evaluator 34
3   Radical Minimalism and Survive Minimalism: two alternatives ... 37
4   Relevance, Neurological Optimization and Language Design 43

Chapter 2: The Syntax-Semantics of the Nominal Construction 49
0   Introduction 49
1   NP, DP or *n**P? 49
2   Radical Minimalism and the structure of the
       nominal construction 54
2.1   The conceptual-procedural symmetry 54
2.2   A note on proper names, common names and
       semantic interpretation 60
2.3   The derivation of complex nominals: syntax and semantics 63
2.4   Numerals, the Localist theory and Radical Minimalism 73
3   The {D}-Split T relation: Interpretability, Case and Theta roles 77
4   Nominal aspect and delimitation 83
5   Summary 85
6   Appendix: On Russell's "Theory of Definite Descriptions" 86
7   Appendix 2: Remarks on Categorization 90

Chapter 3: Empirical problems 95
0   Introduction 95
1   Possessor Raising and Partitive Readings 95
1.1   *Possessor* rising and *possessed* thematization 98
2   Clitic Climbing within the Bulgarian {D} 102

3	Spanish Relational Adjectives	104
3.1	Group (a)	104
3.2	Group (b)	105
3.3	Group (c)	108
4	Possessives as Locations and the Italian {D}	109
5	A note on affixes	112
6	A note on compounds	115
7	On coinage and derivation	118
8	Conclusion	126

Chapter 4: Conclusion 127

Bibliography 129

Foreword

This study has a twofold purpose: on the one hand, we will present a newly-developed theoretical framework which is inscribed within the "linguistics as science" tradition inaugurated by the Port Royal grammar and continued via Structuralism to the present day so-called "Biolinguistic enterprise". On the other, we will narrow our focus and analyze the consequences the adoption of this framework have for the study of the nominal construction, both in a theoretical and an empirical dimension.

The first part of our inquiry will be driven by the will to revisit the basic ontological tenets and operations proposed within mainstream Minimalist inquiry. With the strictest version of Occam's Razor we can mathematically develop, we will deconstruct the Minimalist machinery and, taking into account other frameworks (mainly Optimality Theory and Survive Minimalism), reconstruct it in the simplest possible way. The interaction between the generative *computational component* $C_{(HL)}$ and the interpretative *external systems* will be reinterpreted in neurologically plausible terms, considering the notions of *workspace* (Baddeley, 1992) and capacity optimization given a limited amount of resources. The nature and justification of the Faculty of Language FL as it is commonly assumed in current work will also be questioned, and dissolved in terms of the interaction between an *ad hoc* working space (biologically characterizable as the result of the simultaneous interaction between the pre-frontal neocortex and specific centers of the brain -D'Espósito, 2007-) and interpretative systems whose legibility conditions restrict the generative algorithm that is, otherwise and under optimal assumptions, free and unbounded. The reader will surely notice that our limitation to the study of natural language is simply a choice, since our framework, which we have called "Radical Minimalism", has the characteristics of a *program of scientific research* (Lakatos, 1978), guiding questions rather than attempting to provide definitive answers. This does not mean that it lacks substantive content, on the contrary, our claims are strong enough to draw a sketch of the structure of the physical reality. Moreover, the number of theories that this program allows to generate is limited by the strength of its fundamental tenets, an aspect regarding to which we distinguish ourselves from current Minimalism (Chomsky, 1995 et. seq.): methodologically, the stronger the claim, the more scientifically useful it is, as either its verification or is falsation lead to scientific progress and not to square one. This is consistent with an Euclidean methodology, which we consciously adopt and adapt to wider purposes.

Regarding the empirical aspect of our study, we analyze particular phenomena in different languages to put the theorems derived from the axioms ruling our architecture to test. It is essential at this point to warn the reader about the fact that we will not present a large number of sentences but just the most relevant examples for the purposes of the illustration of the descriptive, explanatory and justificative power of Radical Minimalism. We fully agree with Peter Kosta (p. c.) in that *"it is not so important to have many examples as it is to have the right ones"*. An important observation to be made is that all examples have been checked with native speakers and so have the analysis and predictions derived from our more general theorems. The overall purpose of this monograph is to provide the reader with new tools for linguistic inquiry, accepting the claim that language cannot be studied in isolation but as part of the physical world. Methodological and substantive isolation will lead to useless theories, and it is our strongest belief that no field, despite its alleged richness or revolutionary character, can survive unless integrated within the widest framework of Natural sciences, as every discipline analyzes a facet of an object. However deep the knowledge of this particular facet may be, it is of no use at all unless within a more general theory of the polyhedron in question. This is our guidance and, we hope, that of future developments in linguistic science.

Chapter 1:
An Introduction to Radical Minimalism

0 Introduction

The objective of this chapter is to present the theoretical framework with which we will analyze Nominal Constructions (hereafter, NC) in chapters 2 and 3. We will present the general features of Radical Minimalism, trying to characterize it so that the differences with alternative approaches are stated as clear as possible. However, being an overview, not all issues will be analyzed with equal depth. Should the reader want to pursue an inquiry along these lines, we strongly suggest look at the bibliography, where other works, dealing with more specific matters within this framework are cited.

1 Radical Minimalism and the Natural World[1]

Radical Minimalism is a program of scientific investigation that was born as a reaction to the direction that mainstream Generative syntax took from approximately 2000 to this day. The development of the so-called "Minimalist Program" took a strange twist after the dawn of the new Millennium: the desire to apply Occam's Razor was still very much present in the introductory section of most works but, strangely enough, a curious series of stipulations and *ad hoc* assumptions followed the simplicity desiderata. In this respect, we share the opinion of Jan Koster, when he claims (Koster, 2010):

> "What follows is born out of dissatisfaction with current Minimalism, the received linguistic paradigm since Chomsky 1995. My concerns are not about Minimalism as a program. On the contrary, I subscribe to the overall goal to construct a theory that makes grammar look as perfect as possible and that relegates as much as it can to "third factor" principles. My dissatisfaction is about how this program is carried out in practice. Others disagree, but my personal feeling is that little theoretical progress has been made since the 1980s.
>
> I emphasize theoretical, because empirically speaking the progress has been impressive. One can hardly think of any topic nowadays of which it

---

1 This chapter is based on Krivochen (2011a) and Chapter 2 from Krivochen & Kosta (in press), although with important changes all throughout. We are very grateful to Peter Kosta for consenting in our use of that material.

cannot be said that there is a wealth of literature about it. All of this progress, I claim, is mainly "cartographic" and therefore compatible with pre-minimalist generative grammar and even certain forms of pre-generative structuralism. Part of the theoretical stagnation is due to the fact that some key problems of earlier versions of generative grammar, as they arose for instance in the GB-period, are either unresolved or ignored. But there are deeper problems, it seems, that involve the very foundations of the field."

In our opinion, these deep problems stem from the increasing isolation in which linguistic inquiry was conducted with respect to other scientific disciplines. Even the strong "biolinguistic turn" that linguistics underwent, there is no real communication between linguists and, say, biologists (proof of that is the fact that almost no biologist understands a linguistic paper and vice versa). The programmatic side of Minimalism was fading away, and it is difficult nowadays to distinguish it from the theoretical side, even though they should be not only different but independent: at most, a program is a set of axioms from which the application of a deductive logics and the addition of substantive assumptions result in a given set of theorems, say, a *theory*. This is the background in which Radical Minimalism was developed.

In its *linguistic* version[2], Radical Minimalism is a theory that pursues the claim that "language is a part of the natural world" (Chomsky, 2005b, 2007) to its last consequences. It was first formalized in Krivochen (2011b) and following works, as a theory that seeks to deconstruct current syntactic theory and build a new, radically impoverished model of the mind-brain in methodological terms, focusing on those modules relevant to language, but applicable to any mental faculty (and, optimally, to any physical system). We will now summarize the main tenets of Radical Minimalism:

(1)
- a) Language is part of the "natural world"; therefore, it is fundamentally a *physical system*.
- b) As a consequence of 1, it shares the basic properties of physical systems and the same principles can be applied, the only difference being the properties of the elements that are manipulated in the relevant system.

---

2   We emphasize "linguistic", because RM, as a program, has many other applications in different fields, like Molecular Genetics, Geometry and theoretical Physics. Examples of such works can be found in the Bibliography.

c) The operations are taken to be very basic, simple and universal, as well as the constraints upon them, which are determined by the interaction with other systems, not by stipulative intra-theoretical filters.

d) (b) and (c) can be summarized as follows:

Strong Radically Minimalist thesis (SRMT):
All differences between physical systems are "superficial" and rely only on the characteristics of their basic units [i.e., the elements that are manipulated], *which require minimal adjustments in the **formulation** of operations and constraints* [that is, only notational issues]. *At a **principled level**, all physical systems are identical, make use of the same operations and respond to the same principles.*

Radical Minimalism has as its goal to eliminate all superfluous elements in representations and steps in operations (see Chomsky, 1998), via *interface conditions*. That is: an element or an operation is legitimate in a module if and only if it is required to generate an effect at the relevant interface. As the reader may have already noticed, this is a module-neutral theory, which is an advantage over orthodox Minimalism, with its narrow focus on the syntax *of language*. We apply the same methodological tools that have been used successfully in physics, biology and cognitive science to the study of language, bearing in mind that any attempt of isolating language from other mental capacities is as fallacious as a purely externalist study of phonological manifestations (e-linguistics, in Chomsky's, 1986 terms). Of course, we are not saying that language shares all of its features with other systems (since, as Boeckx, 2010 correctly points out, we may have one or the other scattered in different systems), but it must be considered fundamentally as a physical system if we take seriously the idea that it is part of the natural world, as Chomsky has explicitly done along the years. We must say at this point that, despite what it may seem[3], there is no *reductionism* in treating the so-called Faculty of Language (in case there is one, see below) as a physical system if we consider that a **physical system** is merely *the portion of the universe taken for analysis*. If we consider that universe to be the so-called "natural world", then, our thesis follows naturally. That is, we are not making a reduction

---

3   We thank Phoevos Panagiotidis (p.c.) for making this objection, and other valuable comments as well.

of biology to physics, but simply analyzing a *biological* phenomenon in physical terms, as a physical system (in which there is no contradiction whatsoever) and, as such, applying the *tools* that have been devised in physics in the degree that it is possible, and without confusing the *methodological* tools with *substantive* elements. Of course, looking for exact correlates between *any* two fields would be irrational in the *substantive* level (i.e, units of analysis, as Poppel & Embick, 2005 correctly point out), but we put forth that the *methodological level* has much to tell us, as we are all working with "parcels" of the same Universe that, we will try to show, are ***identical in a principled level of abstraction***, which is the main thesis of Radical Minimalism. This opens many possibilities for research, in multidisciplinary contexts. So far, there have been important works in this field, like Kosta, Krivochen & Peters (2011), Kosta & Krivochen (2011) and Krivochen & Kosta (in press).

1.1 Radical Minimalism as a model for Quantum Linguistics

Our case for Quantum Linguistics will start from a revision of the feature valuation system, under the light of methodological tools taken from Quantum Mechanics (Schrödinger, 1935; Heisemberg, 1999) whose application in the language field is legitimated by the previous assumptions.

Transfer is the operation via which an *interpretative* system takes the minimally interpretable object from a *generative* workspace after *analyzing* it. This dynamics, in which the objects created by Merge are evaluated by the interface systems and, if legible, taken from the workspace is what we refer to as *invasive interfaces*. The transfer to the A-P/ SM component is what used to be called *Spell-Out*, or *vocabulary insertion* in a DM framework. In a *massively modular* mind, *Transfer* is essential in the interaction between modules, since complete informational encapsulation is implausible if the functions of the central module are split into simpler components. In Krivochen (2010d) we have differentiated *transfer* from *transduction*, taking the former to be the transmission of legible information from one module to another, and the latter to be the translation of information coming from the *phenomenological world* to a given *vertical faculty*, in Fodor's terms. In that paper we also said that as soon as a fully interpretable object (in terms of the interface levels, whatever these are) is assembled in a given level, it is transferred, thus leading us to a non-stipulative definition of *phase*:

(2) P is a **phase in L_X** (a given module or level) *iff* it is the **minimal term fully interpretable in L_{X+1}** (i.e., the module it has to present information to)

This definition is *dynamic* and presupposes a strongly componential architecture, in which the components can "peer into" the transferring module to see if a fully interpretable structure has been assembled after the application of a generative algorithm. No *look back* problem arises, since we do not have a module looking into *its own* past derivational steps, but a module X (L_{X+1} in our definition) analyzing structured objects assembled in module Y (L_X) according to its own legibility conditions. Information is taken to be carried in the form of features (Chomsky, 1995, and much subsequent work), be them phonological, semantic or syntactic. These features are, according to Uriagereka's definition, "valued dimensions" of the form [+/- D], being D a given *dimension* and two possible values, + and -. That is the canonical representation of features and the one we will use for the purposes of the present discussion[4]. Within the Minimalist framework, features were fundamentally divided (Chomsky, 1995) in *interpretable* and *uninterpretable* on the one hand and *valued* and *unvalued* (when entering the derivation) on the other. A feature was not (un-)interpretable *per se*, but depending on the category it was part of[5]. The logics were the following: if a feature F makes a *semantic contribution* in a Ll, it is *interpretable* in that Ll. Thus, [ϕ-features] were uninterpretable in T, but interpretable in nominals since [person / number / gender] are (allegedly) semantically interpretable in DPs, and it is the verb that agrees with the noun, and not the other way around. Of course that reasoning is wrong, since (a) there is no definition of "semantic contribution", and (b) if by "semantic contribution" we take "contribution to the explicature" (*decoding* and *referent assignment*), we are in serious trouble since ϕ-features in nominals, for example, are sometimes tricky, like in the case of *pluralia tantum*. Realizing this mistake, Chomsky (1999) changes the angle and entertains the idea that *uninterpretable* features enter the derivation *unva-*

---

4   For details, see Adger (2008) and Adger & Sevenoius (2010).
5   We must now address a reviewer's comment: "(...) in fact Case was/is precisely such a feature, i.e. one with no *interpretable counterpart* (...)". This is actually a point in favor of our proposal: if a feature has no interpretable counterpart (within the theory), then why positing it at all? Uninterpretability makes sense (if it does) only if there is a concomitant notion of interpretability. If a feature has no interpretable counterpart, then, it is not "uninterpretable", just superfluous.

lued from the *lexicon*. In his view, syntax only cares about valuation, not interpretability. However, we also find problems with this proposal. To begin with, the stipulative character of the assignment of valued and unvalued features to different categories is maintained. Besides, it is a clearly syntacticocentric solution, with no attention drawn to the interface levels and interpretability in the external systems. Unvalued features must be valued by *agree* between a *probe* and a *goal* in order to assure *convergence*. Once valued, the uninterpretable features are eliminated, by means of erasure. Interpretable information, on the other hand, is conserved, since it makes a "semantic contribution", whatever that means. Lasnik, Uriagereka & Boeckx (2005) borrow *Conservation Principle* from physics, and state the following law:

(3)   **1st Conservation Law** (Lasnik, Uriagereka & Boeckx's version):

All information in a syntactic derivation comes from the lexicon and interpretable lexical information cannot be destroyed.

The problem with this law is that it makes use of lexical information taken from a pre-syntactic and monolithic lexicon, which is the norm in orthodox Minimalism, but with which we will not work. However, keep in mind the spirit of the principle, since we will try to "recycle" it later. They go further away, positing a second conservation rule, applying to *interpretable structures*[6]:

(4)   **2nd Conservation Law:**

Interpretable structural units created in a syntactic derivation cannot be altered.

Given our definition of *phase*, we can understand what they mean by "interpretable structural units", in fact, one could easily replace that in our definition without any significant loss of meaning and *salva veritate*. But we will try to introduce a radical change in the way derivations are seen. For that purpose, we modify a bit the conservation laws to fit our presentational purposes:

(5)   **Conservation Principle (first formulation):**

---

6   This principle is reminiscent of Edmond's *Structure Preserving Hypothesis*, but the mention of *interpretability* gives it a more "minimalist flavor".

> a) *Interpretable information cannot be eliminated, it must go all-the-way through the derivation*
> b) *Uninterpretable information is "viral" to the system and must thus be eliminated by Agree*

In this formulation we expect to be covering and summarizing the meaning that both Chomsky and Lasnik et. al. wanted to convey ("viral" theory of uninterpretable features is Uriagereka's).

After having presented all this information, there is still a basic question to be addressed: what is really the difference between interpretable and uninterpretable features? Or, to be a bit more radical: are there *uninterpretable features* at all? Notice that the difference between interpretable-uninterpretable, although subsumed to that between valued and unvalued, is still there at the very core of the theory, and is taken as a primitive, with no explanation whatsoever. If syntax only cares about putting things together, why should it bother about valuation and so on? After all, *feature valuation is an operation that only makes sense taking convergence at the interface levels into account, but in the syntax proper (or "narrow syntax") it is perfectly superfluous*, since nothing "converges" or "crashes" in the syntax.

What we propose regarding all so-called "uninterpretable features" is that they **do not exist at all**, especially considering the proposal made in Chomsky (1999) that *uninterpretability* is concomitant to *unvaluation*. That would be the strong (and optimal) thesis. Instead of a number of features (number that has increased over the years) which enter the derivation valued or unvalued depending on the category they compose, we have a minimal number of **quantum dimensions** conveying semantic (conceptual or procedural) meaning, which adopt one value or another in a *local relation* with a proper procedural head, namely, a *Minimal Configuration* (Rizzi, 2004). Let us analyze what we mean by *quantum dimensions*. Chomsky's feature valuation process needs:

(6)
    a) A *probe*, an *unvalued* dimension in a (functional) head
    b) A *goal*, the *same* dimension but *valued* in a c-commanded head[7]

---

[7] The relation is always head-head, even if we say that T matches features with a DP, it is really matching features with D, and all subsequent operations (e.g., movement) apply to the smallest term containing the relevant head that assures convergence, in this case, the whole DP.

We see a redundancy here, since we will depart from the claim that there is no need for the same dimension to be in two heads just for the sake of feature valuation, the arguments in favor of these operations become cyclical[8]. Our argument seeks to eliminate *Agree* both as a relation and as an operation. If the system is really "free", as Boeckx (2010) claims, then there cannot be any "Agree" operation as currently formulated since it would imply a complication for the theory and a restriction for the possible relations between elements (namely, relations are limited to those between *probe* and *goal*). A constructivist theory needs *Agree* in order to establish the "right" (i.e., convergent) relations between elements, but in our theory, based on *licensing*, such a restriction is regarded as stipulative. We aim at dispensing with the need of having a dimension [D] in two places at the same time (in one of which it often makes no semantic contribution) just for the sake of *Agree*, and having *Agree* just for the sake of eliminating uninterpretable versions of [D]. This is, having an [u-T] in D, for example, is absolutely superfluous, and this will be obvious in our more radical theory, to be introduced further below. This circularity is to be eliminated in Radical Minimalism, where the procedural instructions conveyed by a terminal node in a local relation with a structure license an interpretation in LF without the need of positing extra elements.

Our claim here will be that language is part of the natural world, and as such, it is a system whose physical properties are the same as any other system. We will invoke here Heisemberg's (1927) *uncertainty principle*, which can be better explained from an example:

Imagine we have an electron in a tridimensional space, and we want to know its location. In order to do so, we need to see it, projecting some kind of light on it. This light is projected in the form of a *photon*, a particle with mass. The "problem" is that when the photon crashes with the electron, there is a change in the original location, which remains unknown. That original location (we have taken this magnitude just for the sake of the example, but we could have also worked with speed or trajectory) is taken to be a "superposition" of all possible locations, expressed in the form of a "*wave function*" (in de Broglie's terms). Therefore, there will al-

---

[8] If we take an architecture like the one outlined in our previous works, we would first have a "fully interpretable" RSS and then we would add (un-interpretable) features that would be later on valuated by Agree and erased from the computation (see Epstein & Seeley, 2002, for a discussion on this specific point). That is, for us, a redundant (and stipulative) computation, and plainly inadmissible in a Radically Minimalist theory.

ways be a magnitude whose real value will remain unknown to us. In this kind of physical systems, it is the **observation** that makes the relevant dimension *collapse* to one of the possible states[9]. *Uncertainty is a natural characteristic of physical systems, and by no means an instrumental problem*, taking physical system in its technical sense, that is, any portion of the physical universe chosen for analysis. We take "physical universe" to be equivalent to "natural world", and we will use one or the other indistinctly. Magnitudes (or *dimensions*, to maintain a term more closely related to linguistics, since we are not dealing with measurable elements) are *not* necessarily binary; what is more, *in abstracto* they can comprise as many states as the system requires, which, as we will show later, leads us to a much simpler form of minimalism. **We will express it by using this notation: for any dimension D, [D_X] expresses its quantum state.**

Let us suppose that we have a physical system which starts out in a state α, and changes, over some time, into state α'. Of course, it could have started out in any of many *different* states. So suppose it starts out in state β, and changes over the same considered time interval into state β'. We can schematically represent these two possible "trajectories" like this:

(7) $\alpha \rightarrow \alpha'$
(8) $\beta \rightarrow \beta'$

Since α and β are possible states of the system, so is their arbitrary linear combination **aα + bβ**. What ***Schrödinger's Equation (SE)*** tells us is that given that α and β would change in the ways just indicated, their linear combination must also change in the following way:

(9)   aα + bβ $\rightarrow$ aα' + bβ'

The interesting fact about the above mentioned equations is that *they hold only if no "measurement" is taking place.*

If a "measurement" (say, mere observation) is taking place then we must consider an entirely different story about how the state of the system changes: during the measurement, the system S must *"collapse"* into a state that is certain to produce the observed result of the measurement. The hypothesis is exemplified by Schrödinger (1935) using the now famous "cat paradox", which deserves to be quoted in full-length:

---

9   See, for example, the well-known EPR (Einstein-Podolsky-Rosen) paradox, which inspired Schrödinger (1935) paper.

"A cat is penned up in a steel chamber, along with the following device (which must be secured against direct interference by the cat): in a Geiger counter there is a tiny bit of radioactive substance, so small, that perhaps in the course of the hour one of the atoms decays, but also, with equal probability, perhaps none; if it happens, the counter tube discharges and through a relay releases a hammer which shatters a small flask of hydrocyanic acid. If one has left this entire system to itself for an hour, one would say that the cat still lives if meanwhile no atom has decayed. The ψ-function of the entire system would express this by having in it the living and dead cat (pardon the expression) mixed or smeared out in equal parts. It is typical of these cases that an uncertainty originally restricted to the atomic domain becomes transformed into macroscopic uncertainty, which can then be **resolved** by direct observation". (p. 7-8. Highlighted in the original)

The question to be asked now is: how do we apply this to language?

Our answer will be the following: we will consider language to be a physical system, and therefore, if SE applies to any physical system, it must also apply to language.

The next step would be to put this theory in practice. Let us assume the framework outlined so far and the following quantum dimension: [Case$_X$]. Following the idea presented in Krivochen (2010c), to be also developed in Chapter 2, this dimension comprises three possible "outcomes": NOM sphere (ɸ), ACC sphere (θ) and DAT sphere (λ). All three are possible final states of the system, and therefore the linear combination must also be considered a legitimate state of the system. The dimension *in abstracto* could then be expressed as follows, using SE:

(10)   Nɸ + Aθ + Dλ

As we have said before, this only holds if no "measurement" takes place, in Schrödinger´s terms. We will not speak of "measurement", since Case is not a magnitude, but we will consider that the factor that makes the relevant dimension collapse is **the merger of a functional / procedural node**. What we must take into account is that not only do we have DPs with [Case] and functional heads in interaction in the computational system, but the output (i.e, the resultant state) must also converge at the interface interpretative levels, so our problem is a bit more complicated. As usual, we will focus ourselves in the C-I component. What we want to do now is derive the relations P-DAT; *v*-ACC and T-NOM from purely interface conditions, apart from the argumentation we have made in Krivochen (2010c) in relation with θ-roles and Case, to which we refer the reader. Anything else would be stipulative, and that is something we cannot accept in Radical Minimalism.

1.2 Generation in Radical Minimalism: Merge revisited

Let us give the definition of Merge we have been working with in previous works, and then we will address three important questions, that have arisen in the past decade in different frameworks.

Merge is a **free unbounded operation** that applies to **two** (smallest non-trivial number of elements) distinct (see below) objects sharing format, either ontological or structural. Merge is, on the simplest assumptions, the **only generative operation in the physical world**, applying therefore to linguistic units and atoms equally.

This definition of Merge is system-neutral, as well as most of our claims. This means that either a VP or a complex glucose molecule $C_6H_{12}O_6$ can be generated by the same means: binarity and endocentrism are interface epiphenomena, and the advantages of having a single GEN engine in the natural world clearly outnumber the possible disadvantages. Strong though this claim might seem, it is only natural if the thesis that language is part of the natural world is pursued seriously.

From an *intra-theoretical* point of view, our definition also has some advantages over others. We will now summarize some of those advantages:

- Not feature-driven (Cf. Pesetsky & Torrego 2006 Vehicle Requirement on Merge (VRM): If α and β merge, some feature F of α must probe F on β.)
- No set-theoretical Phrase Structure (Cf. Di Sciullo & Isac, 2008, Panagiotidis, 2010)
- Minimal non-decomposable operation (Cf. Boeckx 2009 Concatenate-Copy and Hornstein & Pietroski's 2009 equivalent Concatenate-Label)

We will now address each in turn, analyzing what happens in $C_{(HL)}$ and then in the interface levels, to put some order in the architecture of the grammar.

Merge, as we take it, is a completely free operation that can apply as long as the objects to which it applies have the same format, motivated by interface conditions (this is, {α} is trivial in the interface levels, while {α, β} is not, as we have said[10]). In FL, we have lexical items[11], and we can

---

10 Boban Arsenijevic (p.c) claims that *"{{a}} is non-trivial in at least one faculty: the arithmetic capacity. Hence, output conditions can't be that bare to favor a binary merge"*. However, our position is that if Merge is considered to be an op-

say that they have the same format (be them "lexical categories" or "functional categories") since they share a nature, they are linguistic instantiations of elements that, *per se*, are not manipulable by $C_{(HL)}$. The only attribute of Merge would be putting things together (what the aforementioned authors call "*concatenation*"), without any restriction by principle as regards the nature or number of objects, since it would be a stipulation. Is *binarity* an interface requirement, then? Yes and no. Binarity is the *simplest-non-trivial* combination of elements, and syntax (in the broad sense) is fundamentally economical: there is simply no point in applying Merge to {α}, thus generating {{α}}, if the latter object is in no way "more legible" than the former. This is what we consider to be the trigger of Merge (and any other operation), *Dynamic (Full) Interpretation* (Krivochen, 2011c, d):

(11) **Dynamic (Full) Interpretation**: any derivational step is justified only insofar as it increases the information and/or it generates an interpretable object.

If {α} is not interpretable, for some reason, there is no motive to believe that {{α}} will be interpretable, since it reduces to {α}. But there is also an interface requirement, related with the problem of labeling, that makes *binarity* a (third-factor) *principled* property of *linguistic* hierarchical structures (Chomsky, 2005b), but not a feature of Merge itself. Because of these asymmetries, in Krivochen (2010b) we have made the (purely descriptive) distinction between *syntax in the narrow sense* and *syntax in the broad sense*. The former refers to the recursive combinatory procedure of FL, what is usually referred to as Merge. The latter refers to the recursive

---

eration and we assume also a *dynamic* version of Full Interpretation that states that *any derivational step must be interface-justified*, that is, the application of any operation must lead to a legible object, to apply Merge to a single object is trivial in any faculty. If {a} is already legible in the relevant interface level, then why apply Merge in the first place? It would be computationally redundant, and therefore far from Minimalist. We maintain that binary Merge is the minimal-maximal non-trivial option. We therefore reject any proposal of *unitary Merge* on interface grounds. Moreover, it is not clear at all that the arithmetic capacity (which we could identify with Dehaene's "number sense") interfaces with some interpretative component at all: this problem has been pointed out by Tegmark (2007), who claims that mathematical structures may not have a corresponding halting algorithm.

11 As a matter of fact, we have *roots* semantically defective and procedural features that make them manipulable by the computational system, but we will use the term "lexical items" for the time being, until Chapter II.

combinatory procedure no matter which module we are talking about (C-I, the faculty of music, the mathematical capacity). Of course, our hypothesis is that *there is only one generative mechanism in the human mind, and that is Merge*, but for the sake of clarity we have found useful to make the terminological distinction presented above. Optimally, of course, the theory should dispense with this distinction and recognize that there is only one operation whose apparent variations correlate to differences in the characteristics of the objects it is manipulating and the interface conditions the generated representation must fulfill, a factor totally external to, and different from, Merge itself.

The second question is somehow dependent on the first, as it makes strong claims on the relations between features within a feature-driven Merge framework. We can analyze a "set-theoretical Merge" as meaning, basically, two things:

a) For α to merge with β in the course of the derivation, α must properly contain β, in terms of their feature matrices (Di Sciullo & Isac, 2008).
b) The result of Merge (α, β) can be set-theoretically described in a topological n-dimensional space (Krivochen, 2012b).

The second option is just a mathematical formalization of Merge, and represents no complication for the theory, whereas the first requires features to be present in elements sometimes just for the sake of Merge, thus constraining the derivational possibilities very heavily. Moreover, the model of syntax it implies is a strong *constructional* system (see also Lasnik, Uriagereka & Boeckx, 2005), which we define as follows:

Constructivist theory: Given a generative system Σ, and a finite set S = $\{\alpha_1...\alpha_n\}$ of well-formed formulae, Σ generates S and crucially **no** α such that α $\notin$ S.

The main features of a constructivist system are the following, in a nutshell:
- Highly specified and constrained Σ (for example, Pesetsky & Torrego's *Vehicle Requirement on Merge*)
- Syntactic well-formedness conditions (GB, EST)
- Each derivational step must be well formed (internal contradiction: strict crash proof. See Putnam, 2010.)
- *S* is stipulative defined *a priori*
- Goal of syntactic theory: account for *S* via (*ad hoc*) Σ

- Interface independent (if well-formedness conditions apply in the syntax, there is no point in positing interpretative interfaces, from a strictly Minimalist point of view)
- Requires a highly articulated UG and FL
- Representational approach
- Optimization by *phase* (stipulatively defined)

On the opposite side, we have *restrictivist theories*, like Radical Minimalism and (most versions of) Optimality Theory. Formally, they are defined as follows:

Restrictivist theory: given a generative system Σ (Σ = Merge) and a set S of discrete units of whatever nature, Σ manipulates members of S freely and unboundedly, all constraints being determined by interface conditions.

To make Σ fully explicit, we take the definition of *concatenation* from Krivochen (2012a):

"**Definition 3:** *concatenation defines a chain of coordinates {(x, y, z...n)W_X ... (x, y, z...n)W_Y...(x, y, z...n)W_n} where $W_Y \equiv W_X \equiv W_n$ or $W_Y \neq W_X \neq W_n$. If $W_X \neq W_Y$, they must be isodimensional.*" [W = n-dimensional workspace]

Turning now to the third question, our hypothesis is that **Merge does not entail labeling**, in fact, **syntax** (in the "narrow sense") **can dispense with labels**. Labels are used to indicate which the head of the relevant phrase is, that is, which element will determine the further computational properties of the fully-fledged phrase. However, we will argue, these properties are not relevant to syntax but to the C-I component in the construction of the explicature. Take, for example, (12):

(12) Merge (love, Mary) = {love, Mary}

According to Gallego (2010: 15) in (12), the system sees no difference between [love] and [Mary], and he wants to formalize somehow that it is [love] that *selects* [Mary], and not the other way around, consequently, labels are necessary *in the syntax*. However, our question is be the following: why would the generative system want to know that there is some "selection" relation if Merge is unbounded and the syntax is a purely *ge-*

nerative engine (not an *interpretative* one)? If we have no s/c-selection anymore, no subcategorization frames in a "monolithic" lexicon, there is no way (and no need) of representing this "selection" computationally. All the syntax can "see" is two elements with a common format (two lexical items in "traditional Minimalism", or, in Boeckx's terms, *conceptual addresses*) that can be put together with no restrictions apart from basic economy considerations. If they *can* be merged, then there is no principled reason why they should not be.

A hierarchical representation of a ditransitive structure in C$_{(HL)}$ could look like this (of course, it is not a complete tree, as we have comprised *Split TP* for the sake of clarity):

(13)

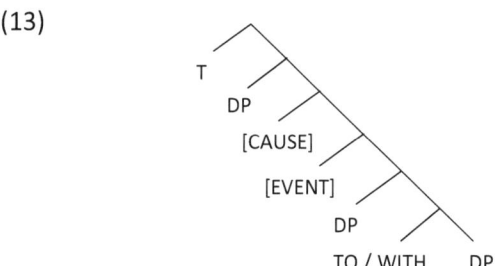

Syntax only cares about combination or *concatenation* (in Boeckx's 2009 sense, we will formalize concatenation mathematically below), because *there is nothing more than a generative mechanism, not an interpretative one*. However, the tree above would be illegible to the semantic component. In order to build an explicature, C-I needs a Logical Form (in Relevance Theory's terms), a subspecified or incomplete representation of the propositional content with procedural instructions to *decode, disambiguate, assign referents* and *enrich semantically* those elements that need so.

Take the ditransitive structure above, for example.[12] If we merge D and P, that is all we do in the syntax, but in the semantic interface there are three options: either we do nothing, or we take the structure to be headed by D, or we take it to be headed by P. Labeling does not really matters to C$_{(HL)}$, because merge is unrestricted *there*, but it is a great way of signaling "headedness" either for the linguist (as a descriptive tool) and

---

12 A thorough analysis of these structures and a justification for labeling is given in Krivochen (2010b, d), and we will not repeat that here, but add new information.

for the inferential component, the post-syntactic instance of C-I, but this does not amount to saying that *headedness* is actually a fundamental feature of language, as Boeckx and others have put forth. Chomsky (in discussion with Cedric Boeckx) argues that "*I don't think that headedness is a property of language. I think it is an epiphenomenon, and there is nothing simpler than Merge*". The "epiphenomenic" character of headedness is given by the fact that it is only required by a C-I requirement, but not by the narrow syntax. Returning to our ditransitive structure, if we "label" the resulting merger as D, all the procedural instructions of P are lost, no relation between *figure and ground* can be established because there is *neither a figure nor a ground*, as they are purely relational concepts. Of course, they do not exist in the narrow syntax, but the relation in nevertheless there, and it is P that establishes it. The same happens when we merge V, which introduces in the derivation an [EVENT] dimension. We can interpret it as two things: an event that includes a spatial relation or an extended spatial relation which somehow includes an event. Interpretation seems to be determined by *scope*, and since the eventive head c-commands the spatial relation, it has scope over it. Interpreting {V, {P}} as P (i.e., a purely *locative* structure) would lead the derivation to crash, as we assume that there is a one-to-one relation between "projections" (in the sense of "labels") and types of information encoded in heads[13]. That is, we cannot have a *single projection* (let us say, for the sake of clarity, a PP) with *two* features of different nature, conveying different information: a P head conveying spatial information relating *figure* and *ground* in terms of *central* or *terminal* coincidence and a V head conveying eventive information in terms of *telic* or *atelic* events. Thus, so-called "maximal projections" can be taken as "informational domains" in terms of interface conditions. That is, when monotonic merge builds an object and that object conveys a certain type of information which the next merged element does not convey, the "projection" is closed in terms of labeling, but this occurs *only because of interface conditions*.[14] The whole picture would look like this (we use traditional X-bar labels for the sake of clarity):

(14)
    a) {D, {P, D}} = P (domain of spatial information)
    b) {event, {P}} = V (domain of eventive information)

---

13 Ergo, we reject proposals for "mixed labeling", like Gallego's (2010).
14 The domains are "contextually defined", and in that sense, they may remind Grohmann's (2003, 2004) "Prolific Domains", but the reader must bear in mind the multiple differences between both theories.

c) {cause, {event}} = *v* projection (domain of causativity)
d) {D (EA), {cause, {event}}} = full causative projection.

We have a note to make regarding the last two points. We have put "(full) causative projection", without any bar-level indication, because we agree with Chomsky (1994) in the invisibility (or, more accurately, irrelevancy) of intermediate projections.[15] The question is: is there any relevance in XP (X'') notation? We think there is not. The [X]P is just a notational form of indicating that the relevant domain is closed, that is, the next head conveys another type of information. *It is a form of signaling the end of a "contextually defined" domain in C-I terms.* Bear in mind that this "label identification" process takes place *post-syntactically*, $C_{(HL)}$ manipulates bare structures like (i) above, whose "parts" are transferred as soon as a fully interpretable object is formed in terms of interface conditions, if the interfaces can "peer into" the syntax and *Analyze* structures in real time (Boeckx, 2007). By these means, we can dispense not only with labels in the syntax, but we can also simplify the labeling procedure for LF (which we will always use in the sense of Relevance Theory) formation. No matter how we indicate it, *v*P, *v* $_{[+ max]\ [- min]}$ or just *cause*, this fully-fledged syntactic object is interpreted as a *caused event that includes a spatial relation*, and we have deduced all this without resorting to stipulations. The indications EA and IA (External and Internal Arguments), which are frequently used in papers on linguistics, and that we have used as well, are likewise nothing more than a descriptive tool, as "internal" and "external" argument distinction makes no sense if there is nothing to be external of in the syntax (that is, if there are no VPs at all and headedness is an epiphenomenon, interface-motivated). EA / IA / Loc, etc. are descriptive terms for (mostly) semantic concepts defined in the construction of the explicature, based on the position that DPs assume in the syntactic configuration, as we have posited in Krivochen (2010c).

---

15 Both Kayne (1994) and Chomsky (1994, 1995) argued against intermediate projections, so that instead of [$_{XP}$ Spec [$_{X'}$ [$_X$ X] Compl]] we would have [$_{XP}$ Spec [$_{XP}$ [$_X$ X] Compl]]. Both had different theoretical reasons and, for us, Kayne's argument is a bit more solid than Chomsky's, since it relies on LCA (assimilating Specs-with Adjuncts). Chomsky simply stipulates that $C_{(HL)}$ can only "see" XPs and X_0. However, the LCA also falls apart if we consider that the syntactic workspace has more than 2-D and trees are nothing more than a model, but not a mental reality.

2 The Architecture of the System: OT, MP and RM

In this section we will compare our version of the architecture of the mental grammar with other proposals, mainly Optimality Theory (Prince & Smolensky, 1993; Müller, 2011) and the orthodox Minimalist Program (Chomsky, 1995 et. seq.). Our goal will be to point problems that those approaches that Radical Minimalism can solve without resorting to stipulations. Our architecture will share some components with OT and the traditional MP, but we will see that both the local and global characteristics of the system differentiate RM from its antecessors.

The model is as follows, without entering into details (from Krivochen & Kosta, in press):

(15)

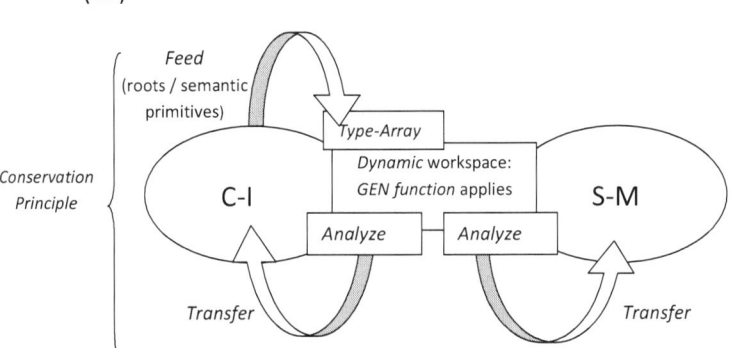

The architecture of the RM-system (see also Putnam & Stroik, forthcoming)

2.1 Dynamic Workspace

The existence of a *dynamic workspace* is quite a strong claim if understood as supporting the "non-existence" hypothesis, which is how we understand it. Our argument is as follows: having a permanent specific module activated occupies operational memory (that is, an analogous of a computer's RAM). Given the fact that the brain has millions of functions to coordinate in less than a second, in most cases, it is likely that computational *working areas* activate *ad hoc*, only when required. This is a claim that extends to all working spaces, with the due note that some are activated more time than others, depending on the stimuli they have to process and the output they are expected (by an interface system) to produce. Narrowing our scope down to the so-called Faculty of Language FL, it follows that there is no FL beyond the convergence of SM and CI, plus the activation of the workspace in this convergence: the prefrontal cortex and specific areas of the brain to manipulate different elements, which leads us to a fully dynamic view on mental faculties, in contrast with most rigid interpretations of Fodor's modularity and following the like of Carruthers' (2006) and Sperber's (2005) *Massive Modularity*. For example, both temporal and parietal lobes activate for Location computation. If we have in mind that in a locative relation the Theme (in Talmy's terms) is interpreted and isolated from the background in the *Temporal* lobes, whereas the Location / Ground is interpreted and distinguished from the Figure in the *Parietal* lobe, we see that what we normally would call a PP (or {P}, in RM terms) is actually a complex structure that involves several areas of the brain.

2.2 GEN = Generator

It is *free*, in the same line as Chomsky's (1995 et. seq.) Orthodox Minimalism and Halle & Marantz's Distributed Morphology (1993)[16]. We will mainly confront our view with the traditional OT generator GEN, which presents some problems: constraints are *global* (in the same way the old Minimal Link Condition was), not *locally* established (Embick, 2010), so an infinite number of inputs is generated for the evaluator EVAL to read (Kager, 1999: 8). In this sense, at least Kager's version of OT is clearly crash-rife (see Putnam & Stroik, forthcoming). Uriagereka's (1998) presentation of OT, though more informal, deals with biological issues that Kager neglects (but see Smolensky et. al., 2002 for a detailed presentation of biological aspects of OT). The version of OT that this author presents is also unidirectional, so that the syntax generates an infinite number of elements, which have to be filtered out by constraints, an overwhelming computational burden. In this sense, this seems to be a crash-rife model. Besides, we could legitimately ask: is *filtering out* a serial or a simultane-

---

16 "(...) *We assume that the Vocabulary of a language plays no role in the creation of terminal nodes at DS. That is, the particular set of universal and/or language-particular semantic and syntactic features chosen for a terminal node is not constrained by whether or not that set of features appears in any Vocabulary entry in the language.* **The bundles of morphosyntactic and semantic features that constitute morphemes at DS, SS, and LF are more or less freely formed.***(...)*". Our highlighting.

ous operation? Serial evaluation would be in tone with Relevance Theory, but the number of options must be reduced, according to a very simple third-factor principle. In this sense, our local *Analyze* step by step is computationally costless, since it is merely evaluating a local unit and seeing whether it fits the legibility conditions of the relevant interface. We will come back to this below.

Radical Minimalism's GEN function is, as we have already said, *Free Merge*, as characterized above. Given this scenario, there are three logically possible options:

(16)
  I. Merge (α, β), $\alpha \neq \beta$ –but α and β share ontological or structural format- *Distinct binary Merge* (Boeckx, 2010)
  II. Merge (α, β), $\alpha = \beta$ *Self Merge* (Adger, 2011)
  III. Merge (α, β, γ...), $\alpha \neq \beta \neq \gamma$ *Unrestricted distinct Merge*

We will now address these options in turn, in order to test them under RM assumptions.

2.2.1 Against "Self Merge"

RM's definition of the generative function Merge allows us to dispense with notions like "Unary Merge" and "Primary Merge" on interface grounds. Let us analyze the following quite from De Belder & van Craenenbroeck, 2011: 11:

> "(...) When an element $\{\alpha\}$ is the first one to be taken from the resource by Unary Merge, it is included into an empty derivation, i.e. the object under construction is the empty set $\emptyset$ (see also Zwart 2010:8). The output of this instance of Merge is no different from any other: it yields an ordered pair, in this case $<\{\alpha\}, \emptyset>$."

Notice that, for interface purposes (the only ones that matter in a "free unbounded Merge" system, since DFI deals with legibility, and syntax is only generative, blind to the characteristics of the elements it manipulates, except for their *format*), $<\{\alpha\}, \emptyset>$ equals $\{\alpha\}$ (which crashes at the semantic interface for independent reasons), since $\emptyset$ is "*completely and radically empty: it has no category, no grammatical features, no specification of any kind*" (p. 12). The application of the operation Merge does not generate an interpretable object, or, at least, nothing "more interpretable" than $\{\alpha\}$ alone (as $\emptyset$ is the "empty set", a Root Terminal Node). Unary Merge and Primary Merge can be both ruled out in favor of simple interface-driven binary Merge by appealing independently to specific legibility conditions (C-I specific requirements to build an explicature) and to DFI, which is a universal strictly interface condition, applicable to *any derivation* in *any mental faculty*.

According to Adger (2011), the basic units with which syntax operates are:

(17)
    a) RLex, the set of LIs, which he identifies with **roots**
    b) CLex, the set of **category labels**

Self Merge combines α and β, α = β, and CLex provide labels for the structures built by Merge. The effect of UM is to create unary branched structures which are extended projections of the root, of the type {...{{{√}}}...}. Besides the obvious criticism that Self Merge is trivial at the interface level supposing that DFI is valid (see above), we have found problems with labels and functional nodes. If CLex is a set from where a function "Label" takes an element and provides an unlabeled syntactic object with a label, some complications arise:

- Potential violation of the Inclusiveness Condition: labels should be recognized, not created.
- Stipulative labeling (there is no principled way of determining the label of an object):
- Label ({√cat}) = N by Root Labeling (Adger, 2011: 12). The algorithm is as stipulative as Chomsky's. Moreover, the introduction of an additional operation is not interface-justified.
- Labels are introduced in NS, where they play no role, instead of *recognized* in the interface. Besides, there is an *a priori* set of labels, whose nature and justification is unclear.
- Labels also take care of *categorization*, which is also unnecessary in NS. No functional / procedural elements are taken into account, what is more, *"there are no functional elements qua lexical items"* (Adger, 2011: 10). In addition, labels may *reflect* categorization, but in no way can they categorize, since they have no entity in NS.
- Functional projections, whose nature is mysterious, are arranged in an allegedly universal hierarchy, resembling Cinque's. One of the problems, apart from no reference to interface conditions, is the following: where (if anywhere) is this "hierarchy" relevant?
- Nothing is said about the nature of *roots*, and the term "Lexical Item" has a strong lexicalist flavor that we would like to avoid.

2.2.2 Against unrestricted distinct Merge

Let us consider the following derivational scenario:

(18) *NS* Merge (α, β, γ) = {α, β, γ}

In the Narrow Syntax, everything would be fine, since Merge is blind and NS is **not an interpretative component**. But, in the interface, problems would arise. Let us assume that α = √ and β and γ are procedural / functional categories, say, D and T respectively.

(19) *C-I$_2$* Label {√, D, T} = ??

Having two procedural categories results in crash at the semantic interface (i.e., the explicature level in Relevance Theoretic terms), there is no way of labeling a structure where two elements could "guide" the interpretation in different directions. The same happens if the numbers are changed, say, two roots and one procedural category: even if we think that one root may be "categorized" (which is not a viable option at all from our perspective), there would still be an uninterpretable element, namely, an uncategorized root, uninterpretable in LF because of semantic underspecification. Binary-distinct Merge, then, is interface-required, no special conditions imposed over Merge itself. In any of the cases, it must be said, the application of Merge involving ∅ (e.g., {α, ∅}) is equal to Self-Merge for interface purposes, thus being rejected in our proposal.

2.3 EVAL = Evaluator

Chomsky's (1995) Minimalist Program had a global evaluator, namely, the Minimal Link Condition MLC, which was soon abandoned in favor of more local constraints (in *phase* theoretical terms, from 1998 on). Too much has been said on Chomsky's phase system (see Krivochen, 2010b for a summary of current proposals and critical readings, as well as our own proposal), and we will not get into it, at least, not yet. On the other hand, OT's EVAL has been explicitly formulated over the years, and consists on a set of hierarchically ordered *constraints*, which apply to representations generated by GEN. It is responsible to filter out representations that do not fulfill conditions established by constraints. There is a competence, as in DM, but not to match the features of a syntactic terminal node (i.e., a *morpheme*), but between outputs that violate as few constraints as possible (optimally, none). These constraints are ranked, which gives rise to a number of problems. It is in the *evaluator* where most of the problems we find for traditional OT theory are[17]:

(20)
    I. Where do constraints come from? Are they part of UG (as some claim)? How could OT manage a non-existence hypothesis, like RM and a strong version of Survive Minimalism, in which FL is nothing more than a dynamic workspace, as we have said above? How are these constraints really represented in the mind, from a biological point of view?

    II. Let us assume there is a number X of constraints. Some of these, say, X_{-4} apply to a L1, and a different subset X_{-3} apply to L2. This is a serious problem, since there are constraints that could plausibly apply to a single language (which takes us back to EST rules). What is more, how can L1 metalinguistically account for the set of constraints that do not apply to it? The development of a metalanguage is problematic (see Kempson's criticism of feature-composition semantics for a similar argument).

    III. Regarding the ontology of the hierarchy, we find the following problem: let us assume that there is a hierarchy between constraints, so that they have the form $<<C_1...> C_2...>>$. Which is the principle ruling the hierarchy? In syntactic X-bar representations, we have the three axioms, mainly *endocentrism*. Here, there seems to be no ruling principle. If there is not, there is a fundamental problem with the very concept of hierarchy. But, what is worse, if there is, then there is an even bigger problem: X-bar phrase structure can be seen as a set-theoretical phrase structure (see specially Di Sciullo & Isac, 2008; Panagiotidis, 2010). If this is so, that is, if there is a set relation between constraints such that C_x cannot apply unless C_y, which is higher in the hierarchy, then the application of the most specific constraint can appear *instead* of long chains of constraints. This would work in the same way as simplifying rules like [+ concrete], [+ animate], [+ human] simply as [+ human], since it presupposes (as it requires) the other two. If there is a true hierarchy, things should work this way, and many constraints could be eliminated in favor of the most specific ones. But the drawback would be that the more specific the

---

17 Needless to say, these critics also apply (with due but minor changes) to the Minimalist feature system. However, we have already criticized it in previous publications, to which we refer the reader.

constraint, the less likely it be universal. So, *elimination of redundancy*, which would be desirable in any system, is apparently fatal for an OT evaluator.

In OT, the EVAL function is in charge of filtering out illegitimate representations generated by GEN. That evaluation, in most current versions of OT, applies at a global level (see Embick, 2010 for discussion), even though *globalism does not necessarily follow from an OT-like architecture*. The main problem we see here is that global evaluation is both computationally inefficient and biologically implausible. If we consider OT-like constraints in a local domain, things get only a little better: the problems with the ontology of the hierarchy remain. What we propose is the following: given the fact that FL is nothing more than a workspace originated from the intersection of two systems (CI / SM) and the activation of the prefrontal cortex, it exists *within* those systems. Therefore, it is only natural that the so-called "external systems" (which are not external at all, in our proposal) can have access to the derivational steps. What is more, we have claimed that it is interface legibility requirements that trigger GEN (i.e., Merge), and we have dismissed otherwise logical possibilities (Self Merge and Unrestricted distinct Merge) with basis on interface conditions on interpretation. The interfaces *Analyze* the result of each derivational step, which only they can trigger, and try to find minimal portions of legible / relevant information. Let us call those minimal **fully interpretable** units *phases*, following Krivochen's (2010b, 2011d) definition, as we have done above. The evaluation is performed by both "performance systems" separately, which has as a consequence the fact that **PF-phases and LF-phases do not need to coincide**. Once one of these units is found *in-real-time*, it is *Transferred*, that is, the relevant interface takes the piece of information and stores it to perform further computations (e.g., reconstruction effects in C-I). This situation of independent evaluation, we will call *Asymmetry* between the interfaces.

The resulting derivational dynamics from what we have said above is as follows:

(21)

Narrow Syntax: Merge $(\alpha, \beta) = \{\alpha, \beta\}$

C-I: Label recognition: $\{\alpha, \{\alpha, \beta\}\}$

C-I / S-M: Analyze: is $\{\alpha, \{\alpha, \beta\}\}$ fully interpretable in the relevant system?

[*C-I / S-M* Transfer $\{\alpha\}$ *iff* it is]

3 Radical Minimalism and Survive Minimalism: two alternatives

In this section we will compare and contrast two non-orthodox approaches to syntax: our own Radical Minimalism and Stroik's (2009) and Putnam & Stroik's (forthcoming) Survive Minimalism. Both approaches claim that the computational system exists in the interfaces, and try to find a *principled*, interface-based explanation to linguistic phenomena, without resorting to stipulations or *ad hoc* elements (Cf. the proliferation of operation-trigger features since Chomsky, 1995). We will present Putnam & Stroik's architecture of the grammar and then point out the differences with our approach:

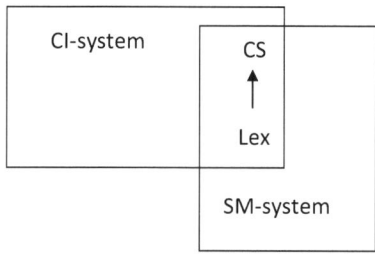

There are some problems that we find with this representation, which we will address in order. To begin with, if the Computational System CS is *within* the intersection of the interface systems, then there is no way of explaining why other cognitive systems show language-like properties, like recursion, unless adopting a dynamic view like ours, in which there is a workspace in which a *universally-available* operation Merge applies freely, as stated in the Strong Radically Minimalist Thesis. The presence of the *lexicon* LEX is also conflictive: there's evidence for *separationism* (Halle & Marantz, 1993, Marantz, 1997, among many others), and following that path, LEX has nothing to do with CI, as it has illegible features for it (namely, phonological features), accepting a monolithic LEX. If LEX is not monolithic, as RM claims, then there is no point in actually positing its existence, since C-I provides semantic (both conceptual and procedural) substance, whereas S-M provides phonological matrices to be inserted in syntactic terminal nodes when *PF-Analyze* recognizes a fully interpretable unit (i.e., a segment that can be Spelled-Out, following some basic Nanosyntax claims. See Starke, 2011 for details). Our *interface asymmetry*, which drastically separates phonologically and semantically relevant dimensions (having eliminated so-called "formal features") confronts with Putnam & Stroik's claim that:

> "(...) linguistic units possess both SM features and CI features. Importantly, these features do not remain separated, as their signifier and signified equivalents do for Saussure; rather they commingle. If we use the piece of paper analogy, these features are aligned as if on a moebius strip." (p. 12, fn. 10)

Another point of divergence is Survive Minimalism's heavy dependence on a hierarchy of features, which are checked in an order that depends on their place in the hierarchy. This complicates the system in two ways: on the one hand, it posits additional elements, not only the features themselves, but also principles to rule the hierarchy and on the other hand, the operation *Agree* must be resurrected, after we have proven its unnecessary character.

Regarding the *Array* selection, we strongly agree with Survive Minimalism in that it is **not** "blindly selected", but no answer is given (neither in Survive Minimalism nor in any other syntactic theory we know of) to the following question: *Why select some items and not others?* Or, to be a bit more radical, *What impedes the selection of the whole LEX in each derivation?* At this point, it seems inevitable to say that NUM / Array is not the beginning of the derivation, but a middle step. Our *Feed* in (15) above accounts for the fact that syntactic structure needs semantic substance, and the subsequent *Analysis* and *Transfer* entails that semantic substance cannot be computationally manipulated if not structured. This view on the functioning of the system, in which there is a prim itive intention embodied in a semantic conceptual structure, then (optionally) instantiated via Language through *syntax* is in this respect a Kantian view on the interdependence of the generative and interpretative components of the system. The *Selection* from LEX (or the whole array of items, however called) is made according to the *Conservation Principle*, maintaining the information across the whole derivational path, and only performing operations that either generate fully interpretable objects or increase the informational load, what we have called *Dynamic (Full) Interpretation*. Both principles are explicitly formulated as follows:

(22) **Conservation Principle (final version-for language)**: Dimensions cannot be eliminated, but they must be instantiated in such a way that they can be read by the relevant level so that the information they convey is preserved.

(23) **Dynamic (Full) Interpretation**: any derivational step is justified only insofar as it increases the information and/or it generates an interpretable object.

The advantages of a *Radically Minimalist* framework are the following, in a nutshell:

- Σ is free and blind
- No syntactic constraints: well-formedness is determined at (and relevant only at) the interfaces
- Allows local repair of non-convergent units (Soft-crash)
- Σ is driven by interface requirements
- Compatible with a non-existence hypothesis (RM)
- Strongly derivational
- Very local *evaluation* (e.g. *Analyze*), but not *optimization* (Cf. Müller, 2011)
- Domains are *interface-determined*
- No features, just *configuration* to relate constituents at the interfaces
- Only one operation: (External) Merge
- Less elements: only roots and procedural nodes, none of which is syntactically anomalous (Cf. for example, the characterization of clitics within orthodox Minimalism as "XP-heads")
- Only interface-required operations
- Deeper explanatory adequacy, as we take into account both the biological and computational implications of our claims with the perspective of the interface systems
- Non-existence hypothesis: more biological plausibility.

This last point deserves some more development, in the light of Reuland's (2009) claims. For him, the *essential properties of Language* are *Unboundedness* of its syntactic structures (*the recursive property*) and *Dissociation of form and meaning* (*the desymbolization property*). From our perspective, neither is an *"essential property"* in the sense that it is language-specific (and thus would be a good candidate for UG-content): *recursion* is out there for any physical system to use (SRMT), and dissociation of form and meaning is an *interface phenomenon*, and if we consider that C-I and S-M are faculties that have independent existence with respect to Language, then the *desymbolization property* is an *epiphenomenon* for the syntactic component. What is more, a closer look to the architecture of the (Radically Minimalist) Universe leads us to the claim that UG is the *empty set*, there is no FL to begin with. We follow Laka (2009) in her claim

that, for a property / element to belong to UG it must fulfill two conditions:
a) Innateness
b) Specificity

Radical Minimalism only acknowledges the conceptual necessity of a combinatory operation and something to combine for language to arise within the mind. Our point is that neither fulfills both of Laka's criteria, and therefore, UG is an *empty set*. Let us start analyzing the combinatory operation, as we have defined it above, repeated here for the reader's convenience:

(24) **Merge** is a **free unbounded operation** that applies to **two** (smallest non-trivial number of elements) distinct (see below) objects sharing format, either ontological or structural. Merge is, on the simplest assumptions, the **only generative operation in the physical world**, applying therefore to linguistic units and atoms equally.

Mathematically, Merge takes the form of a non-specific *concatenation* function:

Definition 3: *concatenation* defines a *chain* of coordinates $\{(x, y, z...n)W_X ... (x, y, z...n)W_Y...(x, y, z...n)W_n\}$ where $W_Y \equiv W_X \equiv W_n$ or $W_Y \neq W_X \neq W_n$. If $W_X \neq W_Y$, they must be isodimensional.

Where W is an *n*-dimensional workspace in which the operation applies following the requirements of *Dynamic Full Interpretation*, should there be an interpretative interface[18].

If Merge is available in other mental faculties (as seems to be the correct view since compositionality can be found in visual perception, mathematical thought, conceptual semantics and other domains), then it fulfills (a) but not (b), thus not being a suitable candidate for UG. This, even orthodox Generative linguists recognize, for example, Boeckx (2010) adopting Gould's (2002) term *Umbildung*, that is, *recombination*, using things already available in separate biological systems to form something new. If Merge is just "putting things together", with no labeling operation involved (Boeckx's *Copy*, Hornstein & Pietroski's *Label*), then this is a strong biological point in favor of our idea.

---

18 Which is not always the case. Take, for example, the GEN formula $f(x) = x^2+z$. Such a function is never interpreted, which means that generation is never stopped by a "halting algorithm".

Regarding the nature of the elements to be combined, recall we only have *roots* (i.e., instantiations of *generic concepts*) and *procedural elements*. They share ontological format, so, for the purposes of this argumentation, they will be grouped as "elements combined".

In Krivochen (2010b, d) we have already introduced the distinction between *generic concepts*, pure *a*-categorial (i.e., they cannot bear category) non linguistic semantic substance which is used by more than one faculty, and *roots*, linguistic instantiations of those generic concepts, underspecified and *pre*-categorial (i.e., they have the *potentiality* of bearing a category). If *roots* are linguistic instantiations of *generic concepts*, then they are *specific*, thus fulfilling condition (b). Now, are they innate? Our answer will be *no*. Let us think of the mind-brain in uniform terms: this means that whatever faculties we find, will have *analogous* ontogenetic development, which seems to be the simplest option and, as "*evolution is Minimalist*" (Bickerton, 2010), biologically plausible. If this is correct, then C-I must have an initial state, determining genotypic possibilities and a final state, a phenotypic expression of this potentiality. The initial state we will call a *Construal Acquisition Device* (CAD) which, in contact with the phenomenological world, gives as a result conceptual eventive templates, which we could summarize as follows:

(25)
    I.   Unergative: caused, without location
    II. Unaccusative / Ergative: uncaused, with location
    III. (Di-)Transitive: caused, with location

Information enters the mind chaotically, but it is organized in very much a Kantian way, into categories that exist as *a priori* forms in CAD: mainly, *Space* (if we accept that *Time* is conceptualized as a metaphor of space), activating *temporal* and *parietal* lobes. However, the existence of more complex conceptual templates must be posited, as our awareness and understanding of the phenomenological world around us does not limit to *things* in a *location* (be it concrete or abstract). In previous works, we have depicted a theory of semantic primitives, which we will sum up here. Ontogenetically (and, perhaps, phylogenetically), the most primitive category is the *noun*, denoting *things*. Things, however, are not isolated, but related in various ways, the most basic of which is a purely *spatial* relation in terms of *central* or *terminal* coincidence (Hale & Keyser, 1997, Mateu, 2000 et. seq.). We have, then, two categories so far, one conceptual, the other, procedural: N and P respectively. Further up on the structure, a spatial relation between two entities is a static *event*, and we have thus derived *uncaused verbs* (i.e., *Unaccusative V*). Different kinds of unaccusative Vs arise when varying the nature of the P node: telic and atelic, static and dynamic unaccusative Vs. The most complex structures appear when the *event* has an external initiator, which requires the presence of a *cause* primitive. We have now *caused events*, which may or may not include a spatial relation: (Di-)*Transitive* and *Unergative* verbs. Having this conceptual (pre-linguistic) skeleton, we can fill the places with the available information, participants, time, place, etc.

The interaction between CAD and the phenomenological world also licenses the different *Aktionsarten*, and it is here, perhaps, where the possibilities of different phenotypic outcomes may be clearer: let us imagine a "lightspeed world": in such a world, there would be *no achievements*, since, for example, a bomb could "be exploding" in progressive grammatical aspect to the point of being a state if we stretch Time enough. In our phenomenological world, conditions of pressure, gravity in a "local" level, and the physical principles that rule the Universe (Newtonian mechanics and Quantum mechanics, in different levels) determine the development of a species-uniform (within certain limits) C-I, and the "delimitation" of the conceptual continuum (recall Hjielmslev's continua for form and meaning) gives us those *generic concepts* we were talking about above.

If the reasoning above is on the right line, then we can say that *roots are specific, but not innate*, since they are the instantiation of generic concepts that result from the interaction between CAD and the phenomenological world. We have thus proved that UG is an *empty set*.

4. Relevance and Neurological Optimization:

Relevance and (Language) Design

Assuming that there is a FL as a "mental organ" (a module) with biological basis, and has, therefore, the general properties of other biological systems, then, according to Chomsky, we have to look for those factors that come into play in the development of this faculty within the species. These factors are (Chomsky, 2005b: 6):

1) Genetic endowment, initial genotypic state of the faculty which determines the limits of variation.
2) Experience, which enables the initial state (conceived as an acquisition device, in any given module) and leads to the final phenotypic state, one of the possibilities licensed by the first factor.

3) Principles not specific to a faculty, including:
   a) Principles of external data analysis
   b) Principles of computational efficiency, and architectural constraints related to development of systems.

We believe there is a close relation between third-factor requirements, architectural constraints that affect the very basis of the systems, and the principles of relevance, which would strengthen the hypothesis that Relevance Theory is an *internist* theory which works at a *subpersonal* level to provide *principled explanations* of the functioning of the inferential module. It is true that most applications of RT have to do with the area of Pragmatics, but this is not an obligatory thing to do, since, as Leonetti & Escandell (2011) say,

> "(...) procedural meaning is a class of encoded linguistic meaning that plays a decisive role in triggering pragmatic inference, but **it is not itself a part of any sort of pragmatic rules or routines (...)**"

If our derivational model generates a Procedural-Conceptual (P-C) dynamics (as has been explicited in other works, mainly Krivochen, 2011d), it is not because there is a stipulation, but because our syntax is blind and unbounded, and constraints are third-factor principles. As there has been no clarification regarding the nature of these principles in Generative Grammar, we think a biologically-(third-factor)based, computationally explicit version of RT can provide significant insight into the operations that take place at C-I, and the three factors model is a very powerful tool even if RM explicitly rejects the existence of FL in the Chomskyan sense. Let us expand on the aforementioned derivational P-C dynamics.

We take roots to have a **conceptually** "nominal" nature. N is the most basic conceptual category, the non-relational element (Mateu's "X") and the conceptual terminal that does not decompose (Jackendoff's [THING]).

(26) N + P = Adj / Adv / V. (Mateu)
(27) $\{_{cause}\ \emptyset, \{_{event}\ \emptyset, \{_{location}\ \emptyset, \sqrt{}\}\}$ = copy of the root's *corresponding* p-signature at PF.

Complex categories are formed with √ (a pre-categorial root) + a number of procedural nodes that cumulatively influence (and determine the interpretation of[19]) the underspecified conceptual content conveyed by the root. We first have an entity (N), then, it is located in space, in relation to

---

19 Escandell Vidal & Leonetti (2011)

other entities (P, establishing a relation of central or terminal coincidence between Figure and Ground). Only after having undergone these periods can we conceive events, first uncaused, then caused, as the latter are more complex. The order of the bottom-up syntactic (linguistic) derivation is *by default* the order of purely conceptual hierarchical representations, built in C-I:

(28) {cause, {event, {location {thing, {location, thing}}}}}

Using traditional labels, this would be:

(29) [$_{VP}$ ∅ [$_{VP}$ ∅ [$_{PP}$ [DP] [$_{P'}$ [P] [DP]]]]]

Does this imply a contradiction with our earlier claim that the C-I$_1$ – syntax interface is not transparent? No. The mirror instantiation is the simplest option, the first to be considered if we take the **First Principle of Relevance** to be valid. Other orderings are later-accessed options, nonetheless available for the system.

Ontogenetically, nouns are acquired first, and the holophrastic period in language acquisition is largely (if not entirely) based on Ns.

Syntax can maintain a root in its ψ-state for as long as it is needed, since it is blind to the internal characteristics of the elements it manipulates, it is only sensitive to their *format*. Therefore, *"uncategorized" roots can be manipulated by the syntax*. Distributed Morphology's *Categorization Assumption* is actually a *semantic interface* requirement, at best, which can be reformulated as follows:

Categorization Assumption (revised version)
No root can reach the semantic interface without being under within the area of influence of a suitable procedural head (D, T, P).

Roots are semantically underspecified, *no less than generic concepts*, but manipulable by the Narrow Syntax (NS). All that changes is *format*, following the *Conservation Principle*. Conceptual content is malleable because it is **fundamentally generic**, whereas procedural instructions are not. The function of procedural elements is to restrict the reference (in a wide sense, nominal as well as eventive) of roots –therefore "guiding" the interpretation-, in order to do which they must have scope over them. Procedural rigidity (Escandell & Leonetti, 2011) is *interface-required*, and we have accounted for that in our *interface-labeling theory*. Let us assume we have a root and a procedural node D. Assuming that the label of {α, β} to be recognized at the semantic interface level must be **either α or β** (which seems to be the simplest option), the derivation could go either of the following ways:

(30)
    a) *Narrow Syntax:* Merge (√, D) = {√, D}
    b) *C-I$_2$:* Label {√, D} = {√, {√, D}}

Or

    c) *C-I$_2$:* Label {√, D} = {D, {√, D}}

Of course, (b) collapses in the explicature level. Roots are way too underspecified to undergo referent assignment, and thus an explicature cannot be built. On the other hand, if we let D be the "label" in the interpretative component, the whole structure is interpreted as a specified entity, because of the rigidity of D's procedural instructions. "Ill-formations", therefore, are *interface-determined*; NS has nothing to do with them. Let us see a more extreme case:

(31)
    a) *Narrow Syntax*: Merge (D, T) = {D, T}
    b) *C-I$_2$:* Label {D, T} = {D, {D, T}} / {T, {D, T}}

Both labeling alternatives collapse, as it is obvious. There is no way of building an explicature out of that structure, no matter how C-I$_2$ tries to interpret it. *Optimal Relevance cannot possibly be achieved*, in other words. It is obvious as well that there is nothing wrong with {D, T} in the NS, as Merge is blind, free and unbounded[20]. Any restrictions are interface-imposed, third-factor legibility principles. This is a way of giving principled status to Grimshaw's claim (traceable to Abney's influential PhD thesis) that *extended projections* always have a *lexical head*, bearing in mind, as we do, that *headedness is an epiphenomenon*, of no relevance to syntax (see Chomsky's discussion with Cedric Boeckx, 2009). We have already described the emergency of "lexical categories", so this follows straightforwardly.

Elements entering NS depend on the RSS (assembled in C-I$_1$) and the *Conservation Principle*, Merge applies and C-I$_2$ builds a fully fledged explicature out of the LF that is transferred by phase.

---

20 This is why there is no point in positing instructions that *"apply at the level of syntactic computation"* (*Op. Cit.* p. 3): syntax (i.e., Merge) is purely generative, not interpretative. Any attempt to codify instructions for the syntactic component would lead to a constructivist system, of the kind we have criticized because of its essentially stipulative character.

Nothing prevents using *naturalistic* methodology in this research, and so our version of Relevance Theory can become a perfect complement to the generative model, traditionally focused on the computational system. What is more, we believe that the very formulation of the Principles of Relevance legitimates this possibility.

The First Principle of Relevance, which makes a strong claim respect for the role of optimization of computations in the mental modules (without specifying a particular, note that says "human cognition", not "this or that faculty"), would correspond to the factor (3b), non-specific principles of economy of a power which come to determine the nature of the acquired language (Chomsky, 2005b: 6). Its formulation is as follows:

Cognitive Principle of Relevance

Human cognition tends to be geared to the maximization of relevance (by biological adaptation, Manuel Leonetti, p.c.)

This is a powerful claim on economy principles, since Relevance is defined as a cost-benefit relation. In any mental process, then, there will be Relevance if the benefit is higher than the cost. In our terms, if the interface effects justify extra steps in the derivation or extra elements in representations. Notice that we integrate and explain motivations for, for example, Movement (understood as Remerge) without resorting to features or other stipulations, but only to third factor principles. The Second Principle of Relevance, which is formulated as follows:

Second Principle of Relevance:

Every ostensive stimulus carries the presumption of optimal relevance

Corresponds, we believe, with the factor (3a), since it is a principle that involves an assumption about external data, be it linguistic or not.

In deciding between different possibilities in a given interface, Relevance Theory is guided by the following principles, defined in Carston (1998):

> "a) Set up all the possibilities, compare them and choose the best one(s) (according to some criterion/a)

b) Select an initial hypothesis, test it to see if it meets some criterion/a; if it does, accept it and stop there; if it doesn't, select the next hypothesis and see if it meets the criterion, and so on."

These claims work extremely well as the formulation of the constraints of a Quantum Mind, with some comments: notice that principle (b) works in a Digital Computer, but not in a Quantum Computer: we do not need to proceed linearly since a QC can compute many possible states of the physical system at once. We can improve the explanatory adequacy of Relevance Theory by enriching it with Radically Minimalist assumptions and get as a result a comprehensive model of the interaction between the syntactic workspace and the interfaces, whatever they are (since, as the reader must have noticed, there is no substantive claim regarding units or levels of representation in Relevance Theory).

In such a model, the optimal scenario, and the one we have in mind, is that all operations are interface-driven, and, thus, ruled by our formalized, biologically-oriented version of Relevance Principles.

In this chapter we have outlined the framework we will use in the rest of the dissertation: Radical Minimalism. The main objective has been to present the reader an articulated set of assumptions and their consequences, and the advantages of adopting such a framework for the study of natural objects. However, in the rest of this thesis we will limit ourselves to Language, leaving prospects for physics and mathematics aside (but see Krivochen, 2012a for a geometrical formalization of RM).

Chapter 2: The Syntax-Semantics of the Nominal Construction

0   Introduction

This chapter deals with the theory of Nominal Constructions (NC) under a Radically Minimalist light. Following the lines of Chapter 1, we narrow our scope down and study the inner structure of NCs and how it interacts with other constituents within the limits of the sentence to produce interface effects. In order to make our exposition as clear as possible, we will first present previous generative approaches, from which our proposal stems, pointing out the theoretical / empirical difficulties we find in each. Then, the Radically Minimalist proposal will be developed in length.

1   NP, DP or *n*P*?

The intuitive idea behind the theories about the syntax of the nominal construction is that there is a nominal head (although, as we will see, that does not necessarily mean a "noun" in the traditional sense) that somehow (e.g., via feature percolation to a label) determines the syntactic/semantic behavior of the whole construction: distribution, meaning, and selectional properties. Within Generative Grammar, the existence of a Noun Phrase was first assumed, but only after some years was it justified. The Standard Theory (Chomsky, 1957, 1965) presented the following Phrase Structure Rules (PSR):

(1)   S -> NP PredP
(2)   NP -> (Det) + N + (PP / AP)

At this point in Generative history, headedness was assumed rather than justified, and there was no formalized system of projection, so the notions of "specifier" and "complement" were not still formally defined. Finite state grammars were already behind, but structural hierarchy was not yet formalized. That would only arrive with Chomsky's (1970) presentation of the first version of X-bar theory, in which a set of lexical heads was assumed and three axioms generated hierarchical tree-like structures:

(3)   Lexical heads: N, V, A, P, defined upon two categorial features, [± N], [± V].
(4)   Axioms:
  • Endocentricity: Every structure has a head

- Binary branching: every non-terminal node is binarily-branched
- Maximality: every head projects a phrase unambiguously

Lexical heads were first defined upon two features, [± N] and [± V], which determined semantic and syntactic properties. The system of projection defined by the axioms generated structures like (5):

(5)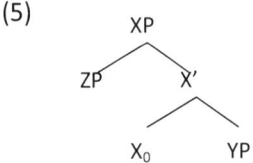

Definitions in this system are circular, even if structural. The center of the definitions is the notion of *headedness*, which is defined as a *terminal node* that is dominated by a *non-terminal node* of the same type (i.e., an X' level). We have already argued against the system of projection and headedness, so we will not return to that (see Chapter 1). In Chomsky (1970), this scheme was applied to all major lexical categories (N, V, A, P) mirroring PSR, giving, in the case of nominal constructions, the following representation:

(6)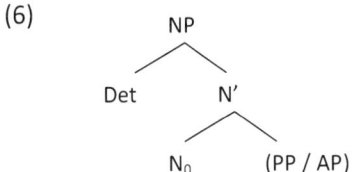

Linear order was not yet a function of the syntactic structure, so the position of complements was not determining for their position in the phonological form. Subsequent developments of the X-bar theory (Jackendoff, 1977) required more levels of projection (like X'''), as empirical problems arose: however, descriptive adequacy was endangering explanatory adequacy. Abney (1987) points out the position of possessors within the nominal construction as a problem, as well as the syntax of *derived nominals*. The solution for the "puzzle" that he found was the proposal that there is an AGR-like node within the nominal constructions, which he first distinguished from, but later identified with, the lexical Determiner. Furthermore, Abney enriched the matrix of lexical features [± N], [± V] with the addition of a new feature, which differentiated lexical categories from functional categories: [± F]. The matrix of the categories we are primarily interested in, then, would be:

(7) D = [+ N] [- V] [+ F]
(8) N = [+ N] [- V] [- F]

Whereas its lexical counterpart, the noun, maintains its traditional matrix, only adding [- F]. This addition created a derivational dynamic of the type [+F [-F [+F [-F...]]]] that is still present at the very core of syntactic research, but in terms of phasehood (see Richards, 2007).

The full extended projection of the DP would then be constituted as follows:

(9)

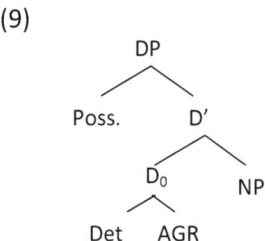

The advantages of the representation at that time were clear: the parallelism between sentence and noun phrase in favor of which Chomsky (1970) had advocated was now total, as there was an inflectional *functional* layer above a *lexical* one:

(10) Sentence: [IP$_{[+F]}$ [VP$_{[-F]}$]]
(11) Noun phrase: [DP$_{[+F]}$ [NP$_{[-F]}$]]

D was taken to be an AGR node with basis on Hungarian data, in which it is made explicit:

(12) A Peter kalap-ja (Hungarian)

the Peter$_{NOM}$ hat$_{[3Sg]}$

"Peter's hat"

Abney's working hypothesis is that nominative case in the sentence is assigned under government by AGR, hence the co-occurence of both agreement and Nominative case. The working assumption is that nominative case in the noun phrase in Hungarian is *also* assigned under government by AGR (as in the sentence), which is "adjoined" to the D$_0$ head (Abney, 1987: 16 ff.).

Besides, the system of selection was simplified as now functional elements selected lexical material both in the sentence level (i.e., IP) and in the noun phrase level (i.e., DP): the concept of f-selection was introduced, and an uncomfortable notion was eliminated from the system: in the NP representation, the head N subcategorized for its specifier D (thus violating the c-command requirement for government and subcategorization), whereas now it is the functional element that selects the lexical one, a move that homogenized the projection system to [X, YP], being X a functional element that licenses YP. S- and c- selection had been already unified by Chomsky (1986b) appealing to the concept of *Canonical Structural Realization*, so the system was now configured around s-selection and f-selection, both encoded in the lexical entry of the relevant element. Moreover, in configurational terms, the "Head-selects-Spec" situation, which was an asymmetry present in the system, was replaced by "Head-selects-Complement", which was at the time the normal and desirable state of affairs. This [D [NP]] relation was also useful for the semantics of the nominal construction, as and lexical layer was assumed to denote a generic entity whose reference was defined and identified by the functional layer immediately c-commanding it.

Eguren (1993) summarizes some other advantages of the growing tendency to consider functional categories as heads of their own projections: more structural places are created to be filled via *Satisfy* at D-Structure, generalizations capturing the nature of both IP and NP were more powerful and principles like the ECP could be applied in both domains, specially within an incorporationist framework (see Baker, 1988). The properties of relative clauses could now be now reflected in their syntax: restrictive RCs were adjuncts to NP, whereas non-restrictive RC were adjuncts to DP, having scope over the lexical argument. The later assimilation of Q and D led to an empowerment of the system, allowing a more accurate representation of partitive constructions as QP-DPs, capturing the part-whole semantics of the construction.

However, the hypothesis seemed counterintuitive (Chomsky, 2007), and the fact that the s-projection of N percolated to the full DP was an argument many used to claim that the relevant head was not D, but N, or some functional counterpart of it.

The "noun construction as NP" hypothesis was explicitly defended in Chomsky (2007), in which he extended the categorization system of Marantz (1997) to the *phase* system, thus assuming that v is present in all constructions, causative or not, because it is the functional affixal categorizer that triggers V-to-v movement to get categorial features. v is not a phase head (or at least, not a strong one), whereas its causative counterpart, v^* is, licensing the merger of an external initiator outside the phase domain. The argument is based in the C-T relation and the phasal status of v^*: just as V is the "visible" head of the v^*P, D is the "visible" head of the n^*P. n would be, again, the categorizer, and n^* appears in causative contexts, for example, derived nominals from transitive / unergative Vs. However, the asymmetries are weak: T, apparently, inherits its features from C, and so does V from v^*. The same is not true of D-N, or even n^*-D. The mere need for n^* to exist is far from clear, since if it bears all features so far associated with D (e.g., referential properties), then D is nothing more than an AGR node (following Abney closely) that bears no interpretable information for the interfaces, and n is the relevant functional projection[21]. It follows from here that n^*Ps are structurally case-marked, undergo subject raising and so on, not DPs. The relevant structural skeleton, given this state of affairs, would be the following:

(13)

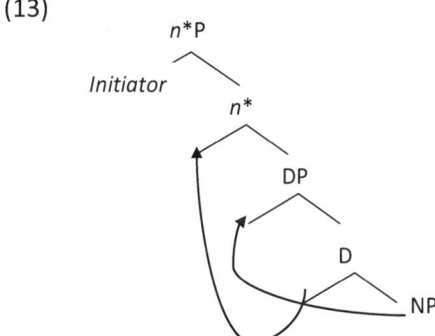

According to Chomsky, D inherits φ-features from n^*, and D rises to n^* just like V rises to v^*. NP rises to Spec-DP, as Compl-V rises to Spec-v^*, in a move that resembles GB's raising to Spec-AgrO and is equally superfluous in terms of DFI. The core idea is, in Chomsky's own words: *"the structure is a nominal phrase headed by n^*, not a determiner phrase headed by D, which is what we intuitively always wanted to say"*. Phasehood is also affected by this new representation: apparently, only constructions with D are phases, consequently, NP does not act like a barrier for extraction or a bounding node, in contrast to what was claimed during the EST years. The

---

21 It is not clear whether pure DPs are "defective" or receive a "residual interpretation", just as bare TPs in Chomskyan models.

n*P representation has been adopted by some (e.g., Radford, 2009), but without much success, mainly because of its essentially stipulative character.

2 Radical Minimalism and the structure of the nominal construction

2.1 The conceptual-procedural symmetry

Before entering the specific domain of the syntax of the nominal constructions, we must make some observations regarding their semantics, since, as we already mentioned in Chapter 1, it is the C-I interpretative component that drives the syntactic derivation via *Dynamic Full Interpretation*. Relevance Theory distinguishes two types of instructions a certain unit, instantiated as a node in the syntactic structure, can provide the interface systems:

(14)
    a) <u>Conceptual elements</u>: these categories are traditionally considered to denote *generic entities*, either from a sortal (N) or an extending-into-time (V) perspective (see Panagiotidis, 2010). In DM terms, we are referring to *roots*. Roots are semantically underspecified, *no less than generic concepts*, but manipulable by the Narrow Syntax (NS). All that changes in order to make them manipulable linguistic units is *format*, following the *Conservation Principle*. Conceptual content is *malleable* (Escandell Vidal & Leonetti, 2011) because it is **fundamentally generic**, whereas *procedural instructions* are not. This means that conceptual content is plausible to be affected by conceptual *widening / loosening*, aiming at Optimal Relevance, as defined in Chapter 1.

    b) <u>Procedural instructions</u>: these nodes provide the interface systems instructions as to how to interpret the relation between conceptual elements. According to Escandell & Leonetti (2011), these instructions can apply at two levels: that of the syntactic computation and that of interpretation. In our free-Merge framework, there is no point in positing instructions that apply at the syntax, since there is a single generative algorithm that applies blindly, and all specificity arises from the interfaces it establishes with other cognitive domains. Our claim is that, therefore, procedurality is not only *recognized* at the C-I interface but also only *pertinent* at that interface.

Contrarily to conceptual content, procedural nodes are "rigid", in the sense that no *widening / loosening* procedures can apply. The function of procedural elements is to restrict the reference (in a wide sense, nominal as well as eventive) of roots –therefore "guiding" the interpretation-, in order to do which they must have scope over them. Procedural rigidity is not an inherent property of some nodes (Cf. Escandell & Leonetti, 2011), but *interface-required* to build a fully-fledged propositional form (i.e., an *explicature*).

We will follow Escandell & Leonetti (2004) in their claim that D conveys procedural instructions, componentially determining the interpretation of the √ within its domain. Crucially, the instructions D conveys are not inherent to it, but just a *potentiality* that realizes in a specific syntactic context. In Krivochen (2010a) we have proposed that a strongly derivational, interface-driven syntax could benefit from a Split-TP theory, and the referential properties of nominal constructions depend on the local relation between D and Tense, Aspect and Modality, maybe also including D-internal elements like conceptual Zeit and cause / event nodes (see below and Chapter 3 for examples). The basic idea behind the Relevance Theoretic characterization of D is that the semantics of D is *procedural*, and plays a role in the extraction of propositional explicatures via reference assignment. Leonetti and Escandell (2000) make the procedural instructions conveyed by definite determiners explicit as follows: *"build a mental representation of a uniquely identifiable referent"* (our translation). The use of the definite D presupposes unique identification in the *mental construction* of the "context", which is *propositional* and mental in nature. Notice that the characterization is fully compatible with that outlined by Generative Grammar, in which D has the semantically interpretable feature of *referentiality*. Within the definite DP, the presence of N (which provides descriptive content) is essential to interface legibility: the definite D selects (in default cases) one and only one of a kind, and the class should appear in the syntactic structure as the NP complement of D.

Procedural categories are said to "project context" in the sense that propositions can be created *ad hoc* to satisfy Relevance expectations, to the extent that the increase in processing effort does not overwhelm positive cognitive effects. The so-called "existence presupposition" that is thought to be concomitant to expressions with definite article in the tradition of Quine, Austin and Strawson is understood in RT as one of these *ad hoc* inferential assumptions: if the referent is not immediately accessible to the receptor of the linguistic stimulus, the combination of the procedural semantics of D and the *second Principle of Relevance* require the assumption that there exists an entity to which the structure containing the definite D refers in the phenomenological world.

Leonetti (2000) follows Abney the identification of pronouns as D. For him, "(...) both *articles and (third person) pronouns have the same semantics -definiteness as unique identifiability- and they also belong to the same syntactic category* (...)" (Leonetti, 2000, emphasis added). We will follow Leonetti & Escandell in saying that the semantics of D is *procedural*, but with an essential difference: Leonetti (p.c.) summarizes the traditional Relevance Theoretic approach as follows:

*"La pregunta de cómo establecería la relación entre definitud, aspecto y tiempo es muy compleja y no puedo resumirla de forma eficaz, pero en principio no tengo razones para conectar la definitud con los otros dos elementos (en lenguas como el español). La definitud es una propiedad de ciertos determinantes, y da lugar a varias interpretaciones posibles, en función del contexto: una de ellas es la genérica, otra es la específica, etc. Lo mismo sucede con los indefinidos, que pueden interpretarse como genéricos, específicos, inespecíficos (...) Ahora bien, yo estoy dando por bueno algo que tú no aceptas, y es que **un SD es definido si aparece el artículo.**"[22] (12/10/2011)*

Our position at this respect is clear: procedural instructions are underspecified insofar as they are not manipulable by themselves, and procedural nodes are tokens that cannot enter into interpretative computations unless within a bigger structure. A strongly derivational model such as Radical Minimalism, with the focus put on the interfaces and the interaction between elements in the derivation following a *procedural-conceptual* dynamics required by *Dynamic Full Interpretation* necessarily implies that no characterization of the information conveyed by a *phonological exponent* (i.e., a definite article) can be done *a priori*, even less so, determinis-

---

22 *"The question of how to establish the relationship between definiteness, aspect and time is very complex and I cannot summarize it effectively but, in principle, I have no reason to connect definiteness with the other two elements (in languages like Spanish). Definiteness is a property of certain determiners, and gives rise to several possible interpretations, depending on the context: one is generic, the other is specific, and so on. The same applies to indefinite articles, which can be interpreted as generic, specific, nonspecific (...). Now, I'm taking as valid something you do not, namely, that **a DP is definite if the definite article appears.**"* (our translation). Cf. also our discussion of Russell's theory of Definite Descriptions and the link between Spell-Out form and semantics.

tically. The contribution of an element to the extraction of explicatures depends on the local relation it establishes with other nodes that can have cumulative influence over it: in the case that interests us, {D} and Tense, Aspect and Modality. The hypothesis is clear: there is *no* one-to-one relationship between category and procedural instruction in the sense that it can be said *a priori* that a particular category conveys a particular instruction, but procedural encoding is also compositional.

A key issue to consider is that the *conceptual* or *procedural* character of an element is neither determined *a priori* nor relevant to the syntax, but only at the semantic interface, in which local syntactic relations are read off and interpreted. If "syntax" is just a combinatorial mechanism (Merge), there is no point in introducing distinctions in the form of features that are not pertinent in the syntactic workspace.

The relation between conceptual and procedural elements is traditionally said to be asymmetrical, that is, there is a predication relation between procedural categories (PC) and conceptual categories (CC): CC are *logical* arguments of PC, narrowing our scope to nominal constructions like:

(15) El hombre
The man

The underlying Russellian-like form would be as follows, assuming the tradition in analytic philosophy according to which the so-called "definite article" conveys unequivocally unicity and definiteness:

(16) $\exists(x), man(x)$

However, this is an inaccurate representation from both a syntactic and a semantic point of view. In previous works (Krivochen, 2011d) we have argued in favor of the following interface condition:

(17) Conceptual-procedural interface symmetry:

There cannot be bare roots without having been merged with a procedural node or procedural nodes without having been merged with a root at the syntax-semantics interface.

This interface requirement stems from the fact that roots are semantically underspecified, as they instantiate linguistically generic concepts (following CP). Bare roots cannot undergo *referent assignment* (either sortal or extending-into-time), nor can they be enrichened semantically because there is no clue as to what propositional knowledge of the world to activate. But, what happens with *procedural* material? It would indeed be a nice symmetry if, as we stated above, procedural elements could not get to the interface if they are not in a local relation with a root. This follows naturally from the very definition of *procedural* elements: they (sub-) determine the relations to be established between conceptual elements, and how a conceptual element should be interpreted as the first available option (i.e., determine *categories*, perspectives on the semantic content of the roots). Let us analyze a curious case: *demonstrative pronouns*.

Our claim is that demonstrative pronouns are the instantiation of *unaccusative RSSs* with a generic root √THING as *figure* and *vectorial* procedural instructions (summed up as "near", but see below) as *ground*. As spelling that out would add nothing informationally, it is left silent, thus surfacing as *pronominal*. When there is a further specification of the *figure* in the RSS, Spell-Out is *relevant*, as it adds information which can be used to extract positive cognitive effects, thus surfacing as *prenominal*. Let us see the structures:

(18)

Relational Semantic Structure: Syntactic Instantiation:

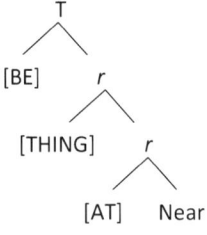
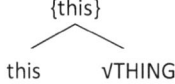

Simple though this may seem, we have missed some interesting facts, so let us get a bit cartographic. There is a curious difference between English and Spanish regarding ellipsis in certain contexts:

(19)
    a) I want those two blue toys. (pre-nominal Adj)
    b) Quiero esos dos juguetes azules. (post-nominal Adj)

Let us ask the question "Which toys did you say you want?" (or something of the sort). The answer could be (d) in Spanish, but (c) is banned in English:

(20)
    a) I want those two blue ∅.
    b) Quiero esos dos ∅ azules.

Is there an inter-linguistic difference regarding the relative position of the root and other nodes (Num, Deg, Gen, etc.) within the {D} structure? Certainly, that would *not* be the optimal scenario, as it would require positing some sort of *"parameter"*, and we have argued against parameters in previous works (Krivochen, 2010d), somehow following the line of Boeckx (2010). Besides, linearization via LCA (Kayne, 1994) does not work in a 3-D model of syntax like the one we propose. We can explain that post-N Adj act in Spanish as *abridged restrictive relative clauses* (ARRC), whereas pre-N Adj are just qualifying Adj, that do not restrict reference[23]. Thus:

(21)
    a) (? In my variety, but it depends on the register) Azules juguetes (the set of blue relevant things and the set of relevant toys are identical)
    b) Juguetes azules (of the whole set of existent toys, just the blue ones: juguetes [que son] azules)

ARRC are enough to restrict the reference of the phonologically null root, so an explicature can be built. English ARRC are commonly PPs or Present Participle non finite clauses, informationally heavy structures that go at the end of the nominal construction. Thus, pre-N (Num, Deg, Quality, etc.) elements cannot assure C-I convergence / legibility, as they *qualify* but do not restrict enough for C-I to identify a referent.

Coming back to demonstratives, their *pronominal* use, as we have analyzed it, show a structure in which all the information is conserved. Consider what would happen if we had posited something like:

(22)

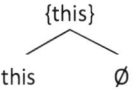

We would have a null element merged with the bundle of vectorial dimensions: *initial point* (0:0), *sense, magnitude* and *direction*, which compositionally with Num_0 and Gen_0 give us *this, that, these, those*. In Span-

---

23 Interestingly, Czech exhibits the same alternance regarding the position of the Adj as Spanish, but it is an exception among Slavic languages.

ish, Gender plays a role along with these dimensions, giving *esto/s, esta/s, eso/s, esa/s, aquello/s, aquélla/s*. This configuration, however, reminds that of De Belder & van Craenenbroeck (2011), which we have criticized: if we accept that there is a RSS underlying these kind of elements, then, erasing all trace of the root would be a violation of the *Conservation Principle*. We return to our previous thesis: instead of [Ø] we have a generic root √THING, whose Spell-Out is *irrelevant* unless further specification is provided[24]. The symmetry between conceptual and procedural elements has then been derived from interface conditions.

We see that the interplay Syntax-Semantics is more complex than current orthodox Minimalism is willing to explore but, at the same time, simpler than Jackendoff's (2002, 2011) *Parallel Architecture* shows.

2.2 A note on proper names, common names and semantic interpretation

In this section we will briefly revisit some long-standing problems regarding the semantics of reference from an interface perspective. Particularly, we will analyze the difference between proper-DPs and common-DPs from a philosophical point of view, and derive the syntactic consequences the adoption of a determined theory of reference has for the grammatical study and vice versa.

A fundamental thesis of Russell's (1905) theory of reference is that if names are actually *definite descriptions* (henceforth, [D]), it should be possible to replace a name for its corresponding [D] *salva veritate*. A "logically proper name", or "name in the strict logical sense", however, is one that has as its semantic value (the contribution it makes to the truth conditions of the sentence in which it appears) an *object*, without involving any particular intensional property. We can take as examples personal deictic items and demonstratives, but in later articles (e.g. Russell, 1917) Russell denied the deictic element the category of "logically proper name", accepting only the demonstratives. For Russell, the other "proper names" in an intuitive and loose sense, are either "disguised" (or "abbreviated" in terms of Kripke) definite descriptions or their existence cannot be assured, consequently, they do not qualify as logically proper names: in the case of a logically proper name, we have secure existence, since its

---

24 This proposal is reminiscent of that of Panagiotidis (2002), but the foundations of each approach differ greatly.

meaning is in itself the referent[25]. If this is so, then a logically proper name could not be replaced by (or expressed in terms of) a definite description, as [D] are defined as a set of identifiable intensional properties. The differences become visible at the level of logical form (in the traditional sense of first-order logics): the logical form of a sentence like "This is a smoker" is $F(a)$, while "John is a smoker" has a more complex logical form, which involves three *statements* ("assertions"), in addition to the theoretical assumption that [John] is replaceable by a [D], such as, for example, (assuming that an individual Z has a neighbor named John) "there is an X such that X lives in the Y building ...". The aforementioned assertions are:

a) Existence (There is at least one X)
b) Uniqueness (There is at most one X)
c) Predication (That X has the property p)

According to Russell, when a sentence contains a logically proper name, such a statement cannot be understood (i.e. semantically interpreted) unless we know the referent of the logically proper name (which necessarily implies that the referent exists, otherwise the logically proper name has *no meaning*). In contrast, by saying $p([D])$, following Russell, we need not know the referent of the definite description to understand the meaning of the utterance, but simply compute [D] as a quantificational expression assuming the three statements and their truth value. In the case of logically proper names, the negation of the existence statement would lead to a logical contradiction, since the very use of the logically proper name *presupposes* that the referent exists (a contradiction roughly paraphraseable as "this thing, which exists, does not exist"), while one may very well deny a statement containing either a [D] or a proper name like [John] in the following sense: "there is no X such that ...", i.e. a propositional function is not true for any value of X (of course, if we take into account the distinction between primary and secondary scope, which is irrelevant in the case of logically proper names, since they are insensitive to scope). The relevant difference, then, is between *demonstratives* and all other names, which are actually definite descriptions. We have already analyzed demonstratives as {D, V} structures, just like any other NC, with the addition, perhaps, of vectorial information on D, such that the lexicalization of

---

25   At this point, the reader must have noticed the inherent stipulative character and circularity of the argument. The existence of an object is stipulated whenever required, so that both the *intension* and the *extension* are modeled upon the author's needs.

the demonstrative is actually a lexicalization of the *module* of the relevant vector, the *direction* and the *sense* being given by the ostensive gesture that accompanies ostension *ad oculos*.

According to Evans (1982), who does not adopt the "logically proper name / other NC" distinction, proper names and full DPs differ not on "semantic richness" but on the extent to which they require retrieval of information from different cognitive sources. In this respect, Evans' theory is very much in the line of Relevance Theory's *conceptual localizer* (from Escandell Vidal & Leonetti, 2000: 5):

> "**Lexical entries** contain information about the linguistic properties of each unit (phonological structure, syntactic category, distribution...) and at the same time give access to a **conceptual localizer** (conceptual address) that gives access to other two types of entry: the **encyclopedic entry**, whose character is representational, containing information about extension and denotation; and the **logical entry**, whose character is computational, and specifies the possible deductive chains"

(Our translation, highlights are in the original)

We see that the differences can be expressed in terms of the instructions proper names and common DPs provide the conceptual localizer, in terms of the lexical (N lexical layer) and logical (D functional layer) entries. Going to the syntax-semantics interface, it must be noticed that, regardless syntactic complexity, all DPs are partial descriptions of the object with respect to the information subjects have in their minds (approximately, Jackendoff's *projected world*), which, in turn, are partial descriptions of the object in the external physical reality (approximately, Jackendoff's *real world*). At this point, we have to conclude that unbounded recursion, which allows the theoretical possibility to generate a structure like [DP [CP [DP [CP [...]]]]] or [DP [CP] [CP] [CP] [CP]...], with infinite referential restriction via Relative Clauses, there is always a degree of uncertainty that is inferentially balanced, provided the accessibility of the necessary propositional context.

Procedural elements, then, *orient* the conceptual localizer towards *what* information to retrieve both within and outside the physical limits of the subject: for example, the [± distal] dimension that demonstratives convey. Needless to say, the amount of procedural information and, consequently, the computational load (in terms of inferential logical steps) depends on properties of the external stimulus: *salience, form* and *internal complexity* (Sperber & Wilson, 1986). From an interface perspective, proper names and common names do not qualitatively differ in interpretation, since, even if it can be posited that proper names do not have roots, it is clear from a historical point of view that they derive from lexical item that have undergone processes of fossilization and coinage. The semantic contribution of the root has been overpowered by usage, but that is irrelevant to the study of syntax and (internalist-cognitive) semantics. A unified theory of reference, then, is in principle possible, not only desirable.

2.3 The derivation of complex nominals: syntax and semantics

Different languages have phonological items that cover different areas of meaning, with a different degree of specificity, as Hjelmslev (1974) very clearly shows in relation to color terms. A theory of D constructions should be able to formalize, first, *intension-extension* dynamics in a language L (restricting our scope to nominal constructions) and then, account for inter-linguistic variation regarding relative underspecification of lexical information and conceptual knowledge. Let us attempt to provide some definitions as *prospects* for such a formal theory:

(23) A lexical item LI is a structure $\{X...\alpha...\sqrt{}\} \in W_X$, where X is a procedural category (D, T, P), α is an *n* number of non-intervenient nodes for category recognition purposes at the semantic interface, and $\sqrt{}$ is a root. (From Krivochen, 2012b)

(24) A root $\sqrt{}$ is a semantic *genotype* (i.e., establishes potentials and limits for variation)[26]. For all natural languages NL, it is the case that

---

26 This could be interpreted as a metaphor, in the sense of Teso (2002): "*El significado es una especie de sustancia química, lista para reaccionar con el contexto que le propongamos (Teso, 2002 p. 44)*" [meaning is a sort of chemical substance, ready to react with the context we propose]. However, provided that we have already the basis for a mathematical theory of syntax in Krivochen (2012b), and biological systems are very specific instantiations of mathematical systems, for which we have also provided a formalization (Krivochen, 2012d), this idea can be implemented as it is. Following the line of Kosta, Krivochen & Peters (2011), if syntax is a biological system (and there is a valid formalization for biological systems, which we think there is) and there is no such a thing as a *sub-categorial / categorial* distinction as in traditional lexicalist models, then the very same formalization we have proposed for syntactic structures understood in the *categorial* level must apply also at the *sub-categorial* level. As a consequence, the entropic biological model we have argued in favor of in Krivochen (2012d) applies to "lexical" derivations as well, since there are only "deriva-

∀(x), x = √, NL ∋ x. Ll in particular NL are *phenotypic* instantiations, and it can be the case that ∃(NL) ∧ NL ∋ x ∧ NL ∌ Ll.

(25) √ are always *types*. Lls are always *tokens* as they are interface readings of a specific syntactic configuration as depicted in (22).

(26) For all NL, and for the set of all procedural elements P = {P_1,..., P_n}, it is the case that NL ∋ P.

(27) Given a *specific* structured set p = {P_1 {P_2 {...P_n}}}, it may be the case that NL_X ∌ p.

(27) is of great importance for the comparative perspective on syntax and semantics. We have the possibility of taking advantage of cartographic approaches to DP like Cinque's (1999, 2001) or Alexiadou's (2001) with methodological considerations of economy on derivations and representations: even if there is a universal set of nodes plausible to appear within the DP (just as there is an allegedly universal hierarchy of eventive / sentential adverbs), a specific combination of those nodes, which is necessarily a subset, might not appear in a specific language L. In other words, even if the nodes are themselves universal, a specific combination might be not. Let us see what such a universal DP cartography could look like, after Cinque (1999), who proposes different functional heads in whose Spec-positions different kinds of QPs check features:

---

tions" in Radical Minimalism, without any further distinction. If this is so, then there is no "metaphor" at all, as in Teso's quote.

(28)

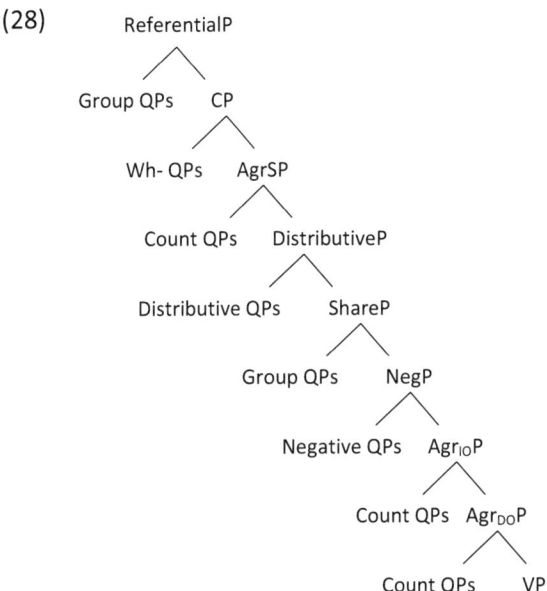

On the other hand, Alexiadou (2001: 19) presents a proposal that is closer to our own, yet still not quite "minimalist":

(29)

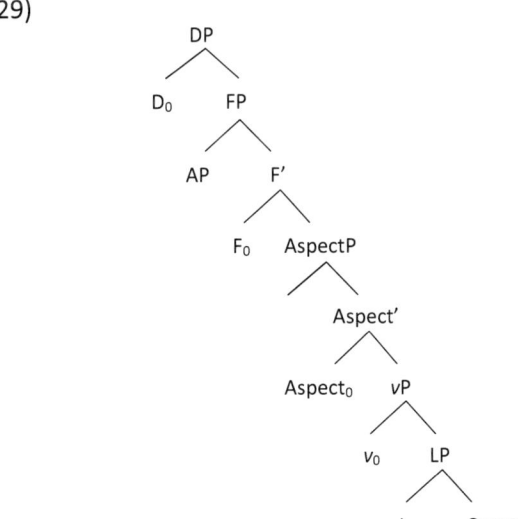

Ticio (2010: 25), building on Grohmann's (2003) Prolific Domains (PD) theory and Rizzi's (1997) Left Periphery proposals, puts forward the following representation:

(30)

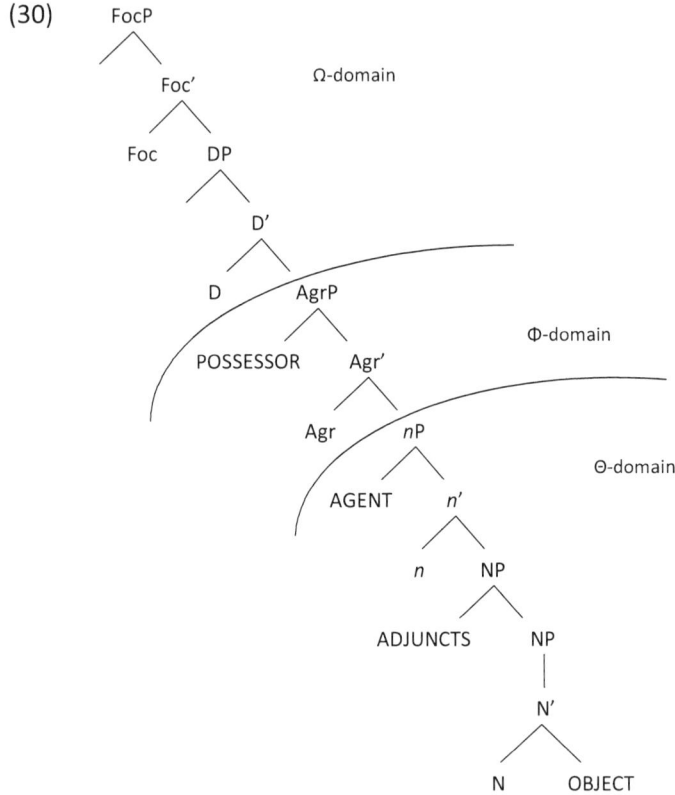

The problems with all these representations are quite the same[27]:

---

27 Ticio's representation has the additional problem of using XP iterations (which are computationally invisible if the syntactic component is indeed purely generative) to indicate adjunction (which is irrelevant in a head-free framework like RM). Moreover, there is no obvious way of accounting for category alternations, since the root involved appears to be categorized from the beginning of the derivational procedure.

- The proliferation of functional nodes whose interface justification as independent projections is not always clear (e.g., FP, AgrP, DistrP, etc.). Moreover, focusing our attention on Ticio's representation, if a PD is to be Transferred after assembled, the presence of an Agr projection would render the whole structure uninterpretable, since Agr projections are mere receptacles of phi-features added *ad hoc* for checking / matching purposes.
- Cinque's representation, particularly, requires a powerful system of features matrices and, moreover, cannot dispense with Agree. From his exposition, however, it is not clear at all whether the position of QPs is *base-generated* or derived via *Move-α*. Even less clear is the identity of uninterpretable features: is it not the case that, in traditional accounts, [countability], for example, is interpretable in QPs?
- The introduction of an LP (i.e., Lexical Phrase, whose head is the *root*) implies that the root has both A-structure (since it takes a complement, which must be subcategorized and therefore L-marked) and some kind of "categorial" feature that percolates up to the label. None of these characteristics is easily derived from a non-lexicalist framework: how is A-structure (which implies an argumental hierarchy) encoded in an element that is taken to be basic and atomic?
- From an interface point of view, it is hard to see how the presence of *all* those nodes (with their respective interface effects, see, for example, FocP) is justified as an *a priori* (functional) skeleton, that is, fixed beforehand. We will focus on this objection below.

The last two objections are general objections to Endo-Skeletal Models (GB, lexicalist Minimalism, DM), in which the syntactic structure is a projection of features contained within an atomic element taken from the Lexicon. However, Exo-Skeletal Models are not any better, from our perspective (last objection): in these models, there is a fixed universal functional hierarchy pre-existing a particular derivation (Borer, 2005; De Belder, 2011). XSM can be seen in action in Cinque's (1999) hierarchy of functional projections hosting different kinds of adverbs: it is implausible that the hierarchy is fixed beforehand (either in the LEX or in the syntax) and, moreover, it goes against considerations of simplicity in representations and is thus incompatible with a strongly derivational approach to syntax like Radical Minimalism. No on-line theory of syntactic generation can allow such rich structures as a starter: interfaces (and our focus, as usual, is set on the C-I component) may require less or more, depending on specific derivations.

We have already stated that, even if a universal inventory of functional / procedural nodes is not only plausible but desirable and mathematically formalizable, it should not (and, therefore, optimally, cannot) be the case that all the nodes appear in all DPs in all languages. Specific combinations are not allowed, depending on Vocabulary Items availability. Such al proposal is a refinement and semantic complementation of our *Morpheme Formation Constraint*, which we repeat for the reader's comfort:

Morpheme formation constraint: We cannot group dimensions in a terminal node (i.e., morpheme) if there is no vocabulary item in the B List specified enough to be inserted in that node.

However, there is an essential difference between PF and LF lexical representations: semantic representations are syntactic, and thus a word (either a N or a V) can convey more or less information depending on:

a) The nodes present in the relevant nominal structure
b) The configurational relations between those nodes

This means that, even if the same subset p of P is present in two lexical structures in two languages NL, the configuration is itself meaningful and thus contributes to the interpretation as much as the conceptual and procedural nodes involved. For example:

(31)
    I. *Reversative reading*: [cause [Neg [√]]] (e.g.: *des-enamorar* [Neg-in-love], from Fábregas, 2005: 269)
    II. *Privative reading*: [Neg [cause [√]]] (e.g.: *des-tronar* [Neg-throne], from Fábregas, 2005: 269)

Needless to say, the considerations above do not imply in any way that the same nodes can adopt different configurations within the same NL, according to different interface requirements. Now, how do we derive interlinguistic differences, to be interpreted at the semantic interface? Maintaining the claim that there is nothing in the inference that is not present is the syntactic structure; interlinguistic differences are to be accounted syntactically. Since RM is not a theory within the Principles and Parameters framework (but see Krivochen, 2012c for an OT-like model of acquisition), parametric setting is not a viable option. Our thesis is the following: all information conveyed by a lexical item (in this case, an N) is derived via *incorporation* (Baker, 1988) of the nodes conveying the relevant information, as long as MFC allows it. This is not a new idea when it comes to V (Hale & Keyser, 1993; Mateu, 2000; Acedo-Matellán & Mateu, 2010), but it is, to our knowledge, relatively new when it comes to N. In Kosta & Krivochen (2012) we have already analyzed the derivation of complex predicators within the nominal construction, such as:

(32) An [A *easy-to-read*] guide

Such a complex predicator needs root-incorporation, in very much the same way in which manner-incorporation structures are derived. Therefore, while in traditional GB and orthodox Minimalism the "valence" of N nodes is taken to be 1 (i.e., one root per terminal node), in RM there is no such a limitation: as long as there are Spell-Out possibilities (either via coined words or neologisms created *ad hoc* following morphological patterns in the relevant language), any node can host a non-limited amount of structure instantiated as a single root, something that is notoriously noticeable in English complex As (as in (29) and Vs:

(33) Yusei also [broke the window] into the room and quickly set up his duel disk. (from www.janime.biz/5DS/series054.html)

Here we see a full thematic domain (in Grohmann's 2003 terms) assembled in W_1 instantiated as a single complex root √BREAK-THE-WINDOW in W_2, an operation that is not different in essence to so-called "complex Spec- Merge", as analyzed in Uriagereka (1999). Our proposal is that what is a full causative node (R) in the RSS level (Mateu, 2000; Acedo-Matellán & Mateu, 2010) is instantiated as a single root in the syntax. This is, à la Mateu Fontanals (2000):

(34)

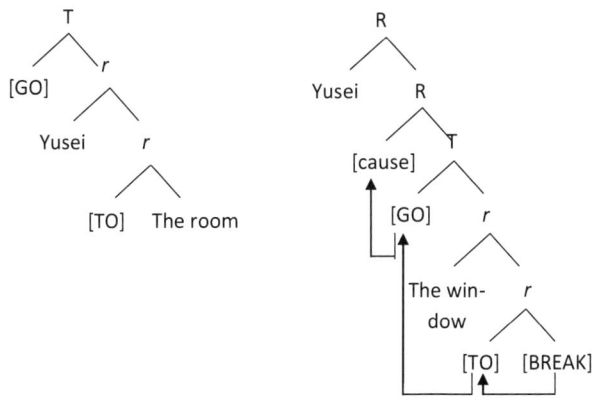

The location structure in the rightmost tree is instantiated as a single root in the syntax, something like √BREAK-THE-WINDOW. This heavy root would be merged with the full {location} structure (i.e., PP), on its ψ-state as far as category is concerned. The local relation with a {Tense} node will do the rest for category recognition at the semantic interface once the structure is transferred.

The same happens within the nominal domain. In this case, the presence of extra nodes in the structure, which is always licensed in a Merge-α framework, provides further specification regarding, for example, the domain to which the referent belongs. Let us analyze some examples[28]:

(35)
    a.   [Das Einbrechen Peters in das Spielzeugwarengeschäft] erstaunte seine Ehefrau (German)
The in-breaking$_{NOMSgNeut}$ Peter$_{GEN}$ into the toys-products-shop surprise$_{3SgPretPerf}$ his wife
    b.   [Włamanie$_{NOM.Sg.Neut}$ Piotra$_{GEN}$ do sklepu] zaskoczyło$_{3SgNeut}$ jego żonę$_{ACC}$ (Polish)
The in-breaking of Peter into the shop surprised his wife
"The fact that Peter broke into the toyshop took his wife by surprise"

The relevant structure of the bracketed constituents in (35a, b) would be as follows:

---

28 German and Slavic examples were generously provided by Prof. Dr. Peter Kosta and Dr. Katarzyna Miechowicz-Mathiasen, and are all normal sentences that occur in everyday speech.

(36)

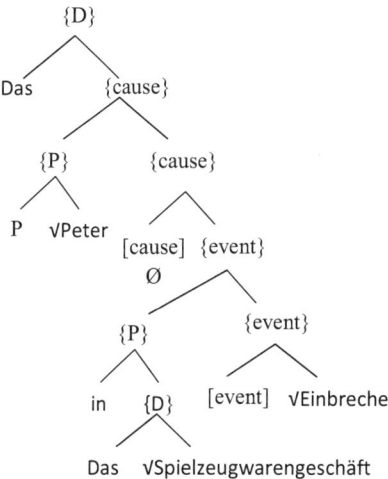

Arguably, [Peter einbrechen in Das Spielzeugwarengeschäft] has assembled in a workspace W_1, and is in turn merged with the procedural node D in W_2, thus generating a "sortal-entity" interface reading at C-I. Moreover, the l-syntactic derivation (in traditional Hale & Keyser, 1993 terms) leading to the coinage of [einbrechen] has already given rise to a new root, as it is very common in grammaticalization processes (e.g., Latin: eo [go] + P = in-eo / ad-eo / ex-eo). Let us, then, explicit the Relational Semantic Structure for this constituent (*apud* Acedo-Matellán & Mateu, 2010), combined with our *n*-dimensional Geometrical model of syntax (Krivochen, 2012b), putting multiple workspaces in practice:

(37)

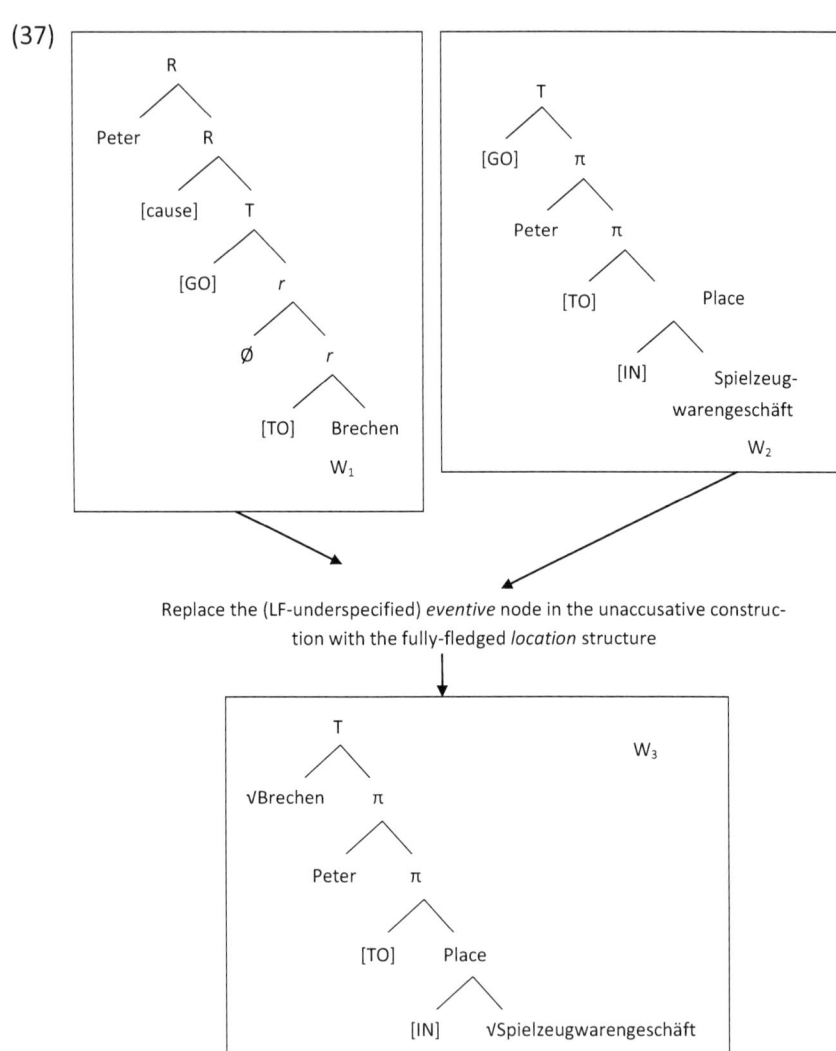

The coined word, then, is *in itself* a POM construction fully assembled in W_3. This shows the potential of GEN and the adaptability of the interfaces' parsing capability. In this case, the π(Path) and Place nodes fuse and Spell-Out as a single prefix, namely, [Ein-]. In the syntactic instantiation, the whole complex structure is merged with {D}, so that, for category recognition purposes, the relation [D...α...X] categorizes X as N. This is an analytic form (as German shows a marked preference for compounds rather than synthetic incorporation), but there are also languages that display synthetic patterns when incorporating information within {D} structures, like Russian or Spanish. For example:

(38) La mujer rubia
 The_{SgFem} woman $blond_{SgFem}$
(39) #La mujer amarilla
 The_{SgFem} woman $yellow_{SgFem}$

This is a very simple but yet illustrative example: even if there is a certain overlap of intensional characteristics (i.e., a range of frequencies within the electromagnetic specter, commonly defined as a "color"), the extension of the terms is not in a subset relation, at least, not with every N:

(40) El pelo rubio
 The_{SgMasc} hair $blond_{SgMasc}$
(41) El pelo amarillo
 The_{SgMasc} hair $yellow_{SgMasc}$

Most native speakers render (40) more acceptable than (41) *certeris paribus*, for a simple reason of specificity: if a language has two terms, one of which is more specific than the other in some respect, and the less specific is used, the extra cognitive effort required to retrieve the relevant knowledge and identify the referent must be balanced by extra positive cognitive effects (i.e., inferences). Otherwise, Optimal Relevance will not be achieved. In cartographical terms, each of those constructions display a different specific subset *p* of nodes, conveying, e.g., domain of application, roughly, *extension*. A specific combination of intensional characteristics greatly influence acceptability, as we have seen. Moreover, if we accept the claim that A is in fact a complex category, resulting from the interface reading of a *locative* [P...α...V] relation, then it is likely that the restriction should actually be formulated in terms of the inferential component being unable to build an explicature with certain *themes* in certain *locations*. Such a restriction could be formalized as follows:

(42) *Given two conceptual entities α and β and an unspecified locative procedural element p, the entities can enter a locative relation iff there p = α ∩ β. If there is no intersection between α and β, no locative relation can be established.*

This restriction is easily visible with extreme cases like:

(43) #The brunette square

However, the disadvantage of our proposal is that it requires a level of refinement in the description of meaning in set-theoretical terms that has not been achieved yet.

2.4 Numerals, the Localist theory and Radical Minimalism[29]

In this section we will focus in a specific kind of elements within the cartography of the NC, which has been somehow problematic for previous approaches: numerals. These elements are specially problematic in Slavic languages, in which they behave as pronouns or adjectives depending on variable conditions. For example, in Polish numerals < 5 behave as adjectives, a characteristic that is said to be inherited from Proto-Slavic (Miechowicz-Mathiasen, 2011c: 2). This characteristic allows them to inflect for Case (NOM, ACC, GEN, DAT, INSTR, LOC; in traditional terms) concording with the modified N. Numerals from 5 onwards have a pure nominal nature, and reduced Case morphological exponents (i.e., only *oblique* cases)[30]. Miechowocz-Mathiasen proposes, in the light of Pesetsky & Torrego's (2004) model, that the source of structural case in numerals is a null light preposition that checks unvalued T in the relevant object. Even though we disagree with the representation and the mechanical part of the analysis (i.e, feature valuation), for reasons already exposed in Chapter 1, we stick to the idea that there is a null preposition in numerals, which amounts to saying that *numerals are locations*. In our model, location is expressed by means of an *n*-plet of coordinates in an *n*-dimensional space, such that a figure-ground dynamics can be formalized as a pair ($F_{X, Y, Z...n}$, $G_{X, Y, Z...n}$), where F is the *figure* (i.e., the object that moves towards or stays in a location) and F is the *ground*, the relevant concrete or abstract location (i.e., properties, states, places). X, Y, Z...*n* are the relevant dimensions in a certain workspace (think, for example, of a Cartesian system,

---

29 The material in the following section is part of a co-authored paper with Dr. Katarzyna Miechowicz-Mathiasen, to whom we owe, among other things, a good part of the theory. We will focus here on the Radical Minimalist side of the question, but see Miechowicz-Mathiasen (2011a, b, c) for details on diachronic and synchronic analysis of numerals.

30 We will not discuss the validity of the so-called Accusative Hypothesis here, since Radical Minimalism's vision of syncretism is incompatible with the current formulation of the hypothesis, and, moreover, the discussion is outside the scope of this work. For discussion and references, see Miechowicz-Mathiasen (2011c).

with only X and Y, now add a third axis, Z and so on: we will get an *n*-dimensional workspace in which to perform operations). This theory allows us to work with a very restricted set of primitives, since relations are decomposed into locative primitives, linguistically represented by the procedural element P. A locative relation, therefore, has the following syntactic form, adopting traditional X-bar conventions:

(44)
```
           P
         /   \
       ZP      P
    [Figure]  / \
             P   YP
               [Ground]
```

The nature of P is variable, following the lines of Hale & Keyser (1993 et. seq): it can either be a *central coincidence* relation, approximately equivalent to the preposition [WITH]; or a *terminal coincidence* relation, approximately equivalent to the preposition [TO]. This variability is a function of the arguments of the locative predicate, such that no relation is fixed beforehand: we have a fully componential system in which relations are established (and relevant) at the *semantic interface*.

Miechowicz-Mathiasen (2011c) proposes the following structure for Polish numerals:

(45)
```
           DP
          /  \
        pP    D'
       [i-T]  D   NumP
             [u-T] / \
                 Num  n/NP
                       △
```

There are some problems we have found in this representation. To begin with, this representation depends on the validity of Pesetsky & Torrego's *feature valuation* system, which we have already questioned as it is simply anti-minimalist. Another problem, even within the theory is that, if T is inherited as Chomsky (2005, 2007) has proposed, there is no phase head c-commanding *p* from which it can inherit T. If, on the other hand, *p* is itself a phase head, then the very notion of T must be redefined, since Ps do not inflect for Tense in any language (contrarily to C). [i-T] in *p* is, then, a mere intra-theoretical requirement, but not a third-factor requirement or some explanatory device required to account for the data in a language

L. A further complication, which we will simplify, is the presence of *both* a NumP *and* the light *p*P. If numerals are prepositions, the very core of Miechowicz-Mathiasen's proposal, then the NumP is redundant as all the relevant information is conveyed by the light *p*. In spite of these criticisms, we adopt Miechowicz-Mathiasen's *numerals-as-prepositions* proposal. The advantages of such a proposal are clear: most importantly, there is a unification of the predication system since all predicates are essentially locative in their semantics (but, as interfaces are *not transparent*, *contra* Culicover & Jackendoff, 2005, not necessarily in their syntax). The syntax and semantics of Polish numerals, more specifically, would be unified. Moreover, the relation between numerals and numbers can be better explained, in the light of recent neurological evidence (Dehaene, 2011) and long-known mathematical regularities (e.g., the relation between the *compression* procedure in the "number sense" –Dehaene, 2011- and the relation between radical hypotenuses in Theodorus' Spiral). The structure we propose follows the line of (43), with a locative primitive licensing the presence of a figure and a ground. The relation between both should follow the lines of our requirement in (41), but this is an implausible claim, as it is. Even if it seems semantically correct to see adjectival predications as the intersection between two extensional sets (*F* and *G*), the same claim does not seem valid for numerals, since a "set of all things that are four" is simply untenable. At this point, either we abandon the idea that numerals are locative predications or we revise the relation between adjectival predication and numerals, refining the requirement formulated in (41). We will follow this second option here.

Mateu Fontanals (2000 et. seq.) has developed the idea that adjectives are derived predicates, product of a local relation between a non-relational element (X), providing the p-signature (Hale & Keyser, 2002) and a preposition, and a further conflation of the former onto the latter (provided that P is phonologically defective):

(46)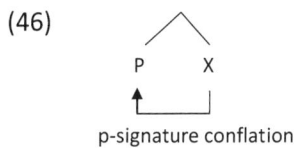
p-signature conflation

This theoretical move, empirically supported, greatly simplifies the categorial system, but it maintains a residue of Baker's (1988) incorporationist framework. In Chapter 2 we have argued in favor of the interface reading of categories as local relations between a procedural node and a conceptual element, plus an *n-* number of non-intervenient nodes for Minimality purposes. We thus dispense with the conflation part, but maintain the decomposition approach. Moreover, we aim at a further homogeneization of the categorial system with semantic basis: if D anchors the generic extension of a root, thus making it a potential referential expression with a delimited sortal entity as "referent" and, moreover, T anchors the generic extension of a root in the Time-Zeit continuum, also delimiting the entity, we would like P to be semantically a delimiter as well. Our requirement in (41) is clearly pointing in that direction, as the extension of *F* and *G* is set-theoretically restricted so that the semantic interpretation of the P structure is the intersection between the sets defined by both *F* and *G*. With properties it is much simpler, but the question that arises now is: what dimension can P delimit so that the result is a numeral expression? Our proposal, in line with Krivochen & Miechowicz-Mathiasen (in preparation) will be that a numeral expression is the result of a local relation between a P node and a generic *magnitude* semantic dimension. This *magnitude* comprises the full array of numbers, which are organized in a locative way (see Dehaene, 2011 for further details about the so-called "number sense"). The generic dimension comprises the whole set of numbers in a quantum manner: a neurologically more accurate way of expressing the underspecification of this *magnitude* dimension. It is, potentially, any numeric expression the human mind is capable of conceiving. This follows straightforwardly from Schrödinger's Equation: all numerals are equally possible final states of the system, and this hypersensitivity to initial conditions is determined by the speaker's intention and grammaticalized via P. The result is the following configuration:

(47)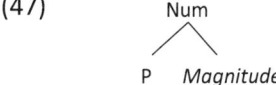

If the *label* of a construction determines how it is interpreted for the purposes of further computations, and provided that we have already dispensed with headedness, there is no internal contradiction in considering that the label of (47) is actually Num. Moreover, the P also determines *where to retrieve information from* in order to locate the N that is modified by the numeral in the numeric space. If this is so, then the nominal in question must be within the domain of P, thus extending the structure in the following form:

(48)

```
        Num
       /   \
      N    / \
          P  Magnitude
```

Of course, and following the line of the theory explained in Chapter 1, a D procedural node is necessary to generate a nominal interface interpretation of the whole structure, since Num is a locative structure with which the interface is not certain to be able to work[31].

3 The{D}-Split T relation: Interpretability, Case and Theta roles

The first question to be addressed if we want to propose a theory of thematic relations, which is of essential importance for the analysis of the NC is what exactly they are, what their nature ir. At this point, we agree with Hale and Keyser to consider so-called thematic relations results of configurational relations, not an autonomous system with its own principles. We do not believe, therefore, they are features (Cf. Hornstein, 2003), as this implies a substantive complication of the theory (the addition of both elements to the representations and derivational procedures to manipulate / compute them) we do not believe is justified. The second question is where (i.e., in which system or derivational point) are thematic relations pertinent or, in the technical sense, *relevant*. Our answer is that they are both read off and relevant *only at C-I*. That is, thematic roles are not part of the syntactic component because they play no role in syntactic computations. Moreover, if the syntactic component is considered to be purely

---

31   This possibility is currently under research.

generative, as we do (and a very impoverished generative component, as the reader may have noticed), then there is no point in positing the existence of substantive theta-relations within W, as the algorithm is incapable of interpreting relations or elements, it just concatenates following DFI.

From GB on, there has been a close relation established between Theta Theory and Case Theory. This link was formalized in terms of the so-called *Visibility Condition*, according to which an element is visible to theta-marking if and only if it has Case[32]. It is useful here to return to the first definition of θ-marking, namely, that a V theta-marks a position if and only if it subcategorizes that position. Considering that there are no predicates that subcategorize more than 3 arguments (one external and two internal), this leads us to consider only three θ-roles at most positions within a projection. In Larsonian terms, the external argument is not within the domain of the lexical V but is required by the functional *v*, the agentive-causative projection that dominates V in unergative and (di) transitive constructions, and internal arguments are actually arguments of P , not V (which is a purely transitional node). Let us consider the following typology of semantic primitives, following Mateu (2000):

(49) Non-relational element: X
 Relational primitives: *Cause* (CAUSE / HAVE)
  Event (BE –stative- / GO –dynamic-)
  Location (TO –terminal coincidence- / WITH – central coincidence)

Those primitives, which we have adopted and adapted from Mateu's work (in turn, based heavily on Jackendoff and Hale & Keyser) can be linguistically represented (e.g., in a sentence like [John made Mary cry], [made] is Spelling-Out [*cause*]), but this does not mean that they are necessarily linguistic. On the other hand, other categories like Tense, Aspect and Modality require a linguistic structure to modify. Let us take Tense: it would be a mistake to confuse linguistic Tense with either physical Time (external and objective, defined as the direction towards which entropy increases) or conceptual temporal notions, what we have called *Zeit* in earlier works (Krivochen, 2012a). Moreover, the conceptual Zeit is expressible in *loca-*

---

32 We will not problematize the fact that, if structural Case is checked in a Spec-Head relation (as in late GB) in S-Structure, and D-Structure is in itself the syntactic expression of thematic relations, then S-Structure should be derivationally anterior to D-Structure, which is an internal contradiction.

tive terms (a proposal that is based on Talmy, 2000 and related work): an *event*, regardless its linguistic instantiation (i.e., a V, a gerundive nominal or a derived nominal) is expressible as an ordered pair (e_X, t_Y), where *e* is the generic event denoted by a bare root and *t* is its anchor in the mental timeline, clearly spatial[33]. Tense, then, is not a viable pre-linguistic primitive, and Zeit can be subsumed to Location. Aspect and Modality, other possible candidates, as they are commonly defined, need to have scope over a defined event (i.e., a {T, V} relation) and a fully-fledged *dictum* respectively, both eminently linguistic entities. As such, to our opinion, they are not candidates for semantic non-linguistic primitives.

Considering that [Cause] licenses the presence of an initiator as external argument, [Event] does not take arguments, and [Location] takes two, we have three possible thematic positions in the 2-D tree diagram below:

(50)

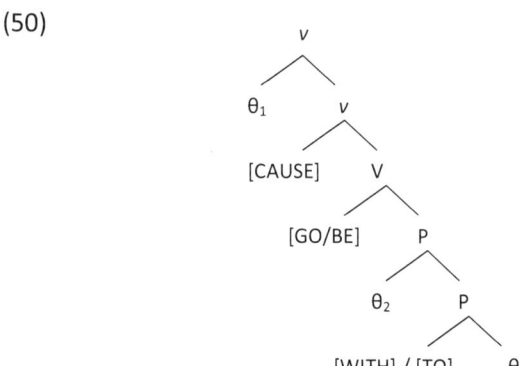

The optimal scenario seems to be to consider a thematic role *per* argumental position. We follow the proposal of De Lancey (2001) to propose three basic and primitive thematic spheres corresponding to the licensed positions, in our terms, Initiator, Theme and Location. Provisionally, we will assume that Initiator is assigned to the position $θ_1$, licensed by [Cause], Theme (corresponding to conceptual Figure) and Location (corresponding to conceptual Ground) vary between $θ_2$ and $θ_3$ depending on the nature of the P node, either central or terminal coincidence. If P is central, then the Ground will be read in $θ_2$ and Figure in $θ_3$, while if P is

---

33 See Talmy (2000) for a recent review of the foundations of Localism, and Dehaene (2011) for further evidence of the localist nature of human cognition, particularly regarding the "number sense". See also D'Espósito (2007) for an overview of cognitive / neural models of working memory, which is essential for the localist theory.

terminal, it will be reversed. All other roles that have been proposed can, in our theory, be subsumed to the aforementioned three thematic spheres. In such a system, further specifications within a sphere are product of post-syntactic inferences, as part of the construction of the explicature[34]:

- Force: Initiator Sphere
- Percept: Theme Sphere
- Experiencer, Path, Source, Goal: Location Sphere

We have outlined the basics of a theory of thematic roles, now we have to see what exactly the role that Case plays in the architecture is. Our working hypothesis is that Case is not an independent system of features, but the result of the local relationship between an argument and a functional-procedural node read off at the C-I interface.

We will work with a system of *three* cases, also structured as *"spheres"*, in close relation to thematic roles. These underlying and universal cases would be Nominative, Accusative and Dative, names that we maintain as a matter of convenience and expository purposes, but we really should talk about an *Initiator Case* (Agent / Force), a *Theme Case* and a *Location Case* (comprising variants of terminal / central coincidence), regardless possibilities of morphological realization in different languages:

- Nominative: *read off* from a {Tense, {D}} local relation, and *interpreted thematically* (in the explicature building process, see Sperber & Wilson, 2003) as Agent / Force
- Accusative: *read off* from a {Cause, {D}} local relation, and *interpreted thematically* as Theme, the object (Figure) located in / moving towards, etc. a Ground
- Dative: *read off* from a {P, {D}} local relation, and *interpreted thematically* as Location, the Ground in Talmy's terms.

An essential claim is that the spheres are not «far apart», but in semantic interaction, and there are *points of contact*. There are elements, uses of the VI corresponding canonically to one «Case» that appear in unusual

---

34   The reader may have identified some points of contact between our theory and Dowty's (1991) *proto-roles*. However, there are fundamental differences: on the one hand, the weight syntax has is much bigger, on the other, we define Initiator and Theme as two distinct spheres, with different licensing conditions. There is simply no way in which, in our system, a Theme can be defined as a non-prototypical Agent, as in Dowty's proposal.

configurations: of these, we will say they are «intersective uses» of the Cases (small dark circles):
(51)

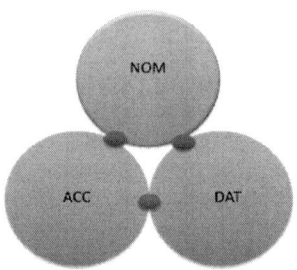

The "intersective uses" include the following (X > Y means "surfaces as X but is interpreted as Y"):

Accusative > Dative: ACC expresses location in space, time or property (i, ii and iii), or goal in movement (iv).
• Direction Accusative:

Latin: Eo Romam$_{ACC}$ (Lit. Go Rome "I go towards/to Rome")

Sanskrit: grāmam$_{ACC}$ gacchami (Lit. Town go "I go to the town")

Polish: idę na pocztę$_{ACC}$ 'I am going to the post office', idź po niego$_{ACC}$ 'go for him (go to pick him up)'
• Temporal Accusative:

Latin: quamdiu, quamdudum, quanto tempore complements.
• "Double accusative" in ditransitive constructions: traditionally referred to as "thing ACC" and "person ACC", they are within the P domain, as *Theme* and *Goal*.

Latin: Verres Milesios$_{ACC}$ navem$_{ACC}$ poposcit. (Lit. Verres the milesians ship asked "Verres asked a ship to the milesians"), Quid me$_{ACC}$ istud$_{ACC}$ rogas? (Lit. Why to-me this ask? "Why do you ask me this?")

Greek: διδάσκω τούς παῖδας τήν γραμματικήν [didáskō toús paîdas$_{ACC}$ tḗn grammatikḗn$_{ACC}$] (Lit. I teach to-the children grammar "I teach grammar to the children")

Sanskrit: rājānam$_{ACC}$ vacanam$_{ACC}$ abravīt (Lit. King some words said "(He/She) said some words to the king")

Accusative > Nominative: ACC is the overt subject in non-finite clauses.
• ECM (Exceptional Case Marking):

English: I want [*them*_{ACC} to come]
Latin: Video [*te*_{ACC} venire] (Lit. See you to-come, "I see you coming")
Greek: λέγει σε ἐλθεῖν [*légei* [*se*_{ACC} *eltheîn*_{INF}]] (Lit. dice te haber venido – active aorist infinitive- "(He/She) says you have come")
Polish: Widzę cię_{ACC} śpiącego. ('I see you sleeping.')

Dative > Nominative: Dative appears in subject position in the Spelled-Out form.

- Quirky case:

Icelandic: *Henni*_{DAT} leiddust *þeir*_{NOM} (Lit. Her bored they "They bored her")
     *Mer*_{DAT} þótti [*Maria*_{NOM} vera garfuð] (Lit. To me seems Mary be intelligent "Mary seems to me to be intelligent")

Polish: Marii_{DAT} znudziła się praca_{NOM}. ('Mary got bored with work')
     Janowi_{DAT} podoba się we Włoszech. ('John likes it in Italy.')

To summarize, our conception of Case is simply a morphological epiphenomenon, parasitic on the syntactic configurations that license so-called "theta-roles". A semantically-driven inquiry has lead us to a substantial simplification of the theoretical apparatus, without overloading the interfaces (since explicature-building is a process that has to take place anyway). Let us graphic the licensing domains so that the configurations are fully explicit:

(52)

NOM-sphere licensing domain

ACC-sphere licensing domain

DAT-sphere licensing domain

{Mod} — [Mod], {Asp} — [Asp], {T} — [T], {cause} — Initiator [Case_y], {cause} — [CAUSE], {event} — [EVENT], {P} — Figure [Case_x], {P} — [TO], Ground [Case_x]

The relative position of the functional elements above {cause} deserves further clarification. The eventive domain and associated projections (i.e., VP, vP, VoiceP, etc.) denotes an event, but generic, without any procedural instruction to anchor it within a timeline. Conceptually, events are entities, and they behave, syntactically and semantically, like nominal constructions. Therefore, {T} should dominate {event} because it is the equivalent of {D}, anchors the reference of the generic event with respect to a reference point, such that the interpretable version of en event *e* is, in the simplest cases of absolute tense, actually an ordered pair of the form (e_X, t_Y), just like the interpretable version of a sortal entity is also an ordered pair of the form (n_X, s_Y), where *n* is a sortal variable and *s* is the spaceline. As for {Asp}, it encodes a decision of the speaker as to present the event delimited by T as a *point* (perfective aspect) or a *developing process* (imperfective aspect). Therefore, in X-bar terms, {Asp} dominates {T}, because {Asp} must have *scope* over the delimited event at LF. {Mod}, finally, is the expression of the subjectivity of the speaker regarding the *dictum* (i.e., the {Asp} domain) in terms of [realis] / [irrealis], which affects the *whole proposition*. If we also accept the claim that at least part of what is considered to constitute the "left periphery" is actually within Mod (as are so-called "disjuncts"), we are lead to consider that this procedural node must have scope over the rest of the proposition, thus getting the structure in (52). {Mod} mod is not just limited to morphological indicative, subjunctive or imperative but also epistemic or deontic elements of whichever grammatical category, since it is the procedural instructions it conveys that matter. Syntactic categories (i.e. "parts of speech", in traditional terms) are interface readings of syntactic configurations, therefore, they are not a system of primitives (Cf. Hale & Keyser, 1993).

4 Nominal aspect and delimitation

In the field of Conceptual Semantics, Jackendoff distinguishes between delimited and non-delimited entities, a distinction that covers all lexical categories (N, V, A, P and Adv). As far as N is concerned, this distinction corresponds to the traditional semantically-based opposition between *countable* N (table, cup), vs. *uncountable* N (goodness, water). These dimensions, however, should also be interface readings of syntactic configurations, as it is not possible to speak of entities inherently limited or not, but, along the lines that we have been developing, delimitation is a componential phenomenon resulting from the interface reading of a local relationship between a node that denotes the relevant class of entities and a procedural node conveying instructions regarding interpretation and delimitation of the semantic substance (see above) which has scope over it. It seems to be the case that the P procedural layer which we have already introduced for numerals is also responsible for determining the interpretation, as P can be delimitative for either sortal or eventive entities. If we were to take only roots into consideration, we would be left with a set of non-delimited objects due to their interface underspecification. If, conversely, we considered only procedural instructions, the situation we have already explained in Chapter 1 would arise: instructions regarding how to manipulate semantic substance are completely useless in the absence of such a substance. It seems that the derivational dynamics of natural language follow a Kantian logic: instructions without concepts are vacuous, and concepts without instructions are blind.

"Delimitation" means defining the boundaries of the entity, conceptualization of the object as a point, homogeneous, without paying attention to its internal complexity. These discrete objects, once delimited, can be, for example, quantified and pluralized. Non-delimitation involves conceptualization of the object as a substance more or less heterogeneous, expanded, without clear boundaries and considering its internal complexity and structure. We propose to subsume the option [± delimited] to [± perfective], which means that the Aspectual distinction is relevant not only on the verbal domain but also on the nominal construction. Quite straightforwardly, we identify *delimitation* with *perfectivity* and *non-delimination* with *imperfectivity*. {D}, then, does not act alone in determining the interpretation, but the interface reading depends on the compositional association of the procedural instructions of D regarding entity identification with other nodes, in this case Asp or P, which have scope over the semantic substance, i.e., the *root* √.

One possible question here is whether *definiteness* is identifiable with *delimitation* (and, therefore, *perfectiveness*). As we have mentioned above, [delimitation] is an aspectual dimension, the manifestation of [± perfective] within the nominal level and not restricted to it. In Krivochen (2010a) our working hypothesis was that referentiality and definiteness are *valuable dimensions* (i.e., not fixed beforehand), and we opposed *definiteness* to *genericity*. Identifying definiteness with delimitation would imply identifying genericity with non-delimitation, which would predict wrong empirical consequences. Although there is a *correlation* between perfectivity and definiteness, it would be a mistake to take it as a strict univocal relation. The generic form can be conceptualized in perfective terms, i.e., as an internally unanalyzable whole: a particular statement is valid for all the members of the species, yet *only* for the species denoted by the generic root. There are limits on the scope of the generic reference. The licensing conditions for semantic interpretation do not follow a strict *a priori* rule, since we can have generic interpretations as the most accessible explicature even with perfective aspectual features and definite interpretations in the presence of imperfective features, as the following examples illustrate:

(53) El tiranosaurio **vivió** durante el período cretácico (perfective features, generic interpretation)
The tyranosaur live$_{3SgPastPerf}$ during the period cretacic.

(54) El elefante **comía** varios kilos de comida (al día) (imperfective features, definite interpretation)
The elephant eat$_{3SgPastImpf}$ several kilograms of food (per day)

A priori, we cannot establish fixed rules for the computation of each concrete example, which will be driven by the need to fulfill expectations of Optimal Relevance in a context: since the set S of propositions that configure the "context" varies as it is selected *ad hoc* for the computation of a linguistic stimulus, any attempt to establish strict principles and invariant correlations in a context-free (i.e., Aristotelian) model of interpretation would inevitably result stipulative, thus incompatible with Radical Minimalism.

5 Summary

The basic architecture for a nominal expression to be interpreted is, then, (55):

(55)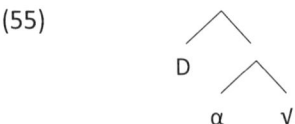

Where there can be a non-specified number of semantically interpretable nodes structurally positioned between the D and the root, but distributionally underspecified so that they do not generate a categorial reading at the interface (e.g., Asp, P, *cause, event*, which can appear in both "derived" nominals and verbs, as we have pointed out in Krivochen, 2011d).

In a more general spirit, the minimal structure of any referential expression (either eventive or sortal) is, as we have already analyzed, (56):

(56)

Where *p* is a distributionally specified procedural node, in concrete terms, either T, D or P. Of course, as we have seen in (36), this structure can be expanded if the interfaces (via DFI) require so, but there is no "pre-existent" functional skeleton as in Cinque's proposals or Exo-Skeletal Models (XSM). Our syntactic component is freer than orthodox Minimalism, but our semantic interface is much more articulated and formalized, by no means a "fuzzy area" where things happen in a mysterious way. The freedom in the GEN component allows RM to account for the data in ways previous theories cannot, due to constraints the framework imposes on them. The potential of our model to analyze data from different languages in an elegant way will be the focus of Chapter 3, dealing exclusively with *natural data* from *native speakers* of each of the languages we have considered.

6 Appendix: On Russell's "Theory of Definite Descriptions"[35]

The theory of definite descriptions, presented in Russell (1905), begins with a categorical statement about the relationship between form and content, a claim which, as we shall see, is stipulative and therefore unacceptable within our framework:

---

35 We acknowledge and thank Dr. Alberto Moretti's (p.c.) objection to our analysis that Russell's aim is not to develop a general theory of NCs, but only of a subset of them, and with very specific purposes. On the contrary, we aim at a general theory of NC, as is the common practice in formal linguistics. However "unfair" our objections may seem, it is also true that the method Russell uses is the "from-PF-to-syntax" path we have already criticized, and, moreover, the influence Russellian theories of reference have in today's linguistic approaches to the problem is surprisingly big. So, our focus in this section is put on Russell, but our critic goes much beyond.

> By a " denoting phrase " I mean a phrase such as any one of the following : a man, some man, any man, every man, all men, the present King of England, the present King of France, the centre of mass of the Solar System at the first instant of the twentieth century, the revolution of the earth round the sun, the revolution of the sun round the earth. Thus **a phrase is denoting solely in virtue of its form.** (Russell, 1905: 1. Our highlight)

Notice that the statement in question contains two undefined concepts: "denoting" and "form". These concepts, defined one as a function of the other, result in a deterministic statement regarding the relationship between form and content, which goes against the strongly componential approach we pursue here. The fixed nature of the function is reinforced by the word "solely" which restricts the denotative capacity, whatever it is, to a particularity of the form: the *interpretation* of a definite description is only given in terms of the elements made lexically , Q / D + N. The use of "form" to refer to the *signifiant* of the Saussurean sign, or *phonological form* in generative models, is very common in Anglo-Saxon versions of Aristotle's Poetics. Note that the denotative phrases used as examples all contain an overt definite article, which is essential for Russell's arguments. We will examine some empirical arguments against Russellian theories of reference, setting our focus on Russell's own (1905) proposal[36].

The logical form of denoting phrases reduces to Q(x), a procedure via which the denoting phrase is eliminated in the paraphrase. However, Russell makes a mistake in the analysis of the quantification involved in [Determiner / Quantifier [N ...]] structures. Consider his analysis of a structure of type $\forall(x)$:

(57) C(everything) means "C(x) is always true"

Which, at first sight incompatible with the following statement:

(58) $\exists(x) \wedge \sim C(x)$

However, formalities aside, this does not capture the actual semantics of the universal quantifier. The problem is evident in languages like Spanish, where there are two available Vocabulary Items, "todo" and "cada". *A priori*, a sentence like (59) is not unacceptable:

(59)   Todos los italianos son gritones, pero conozco a uno que no lo es
       All the Italians are loud, but I know P one that Neg CL_{ACC} is

---

36   For a comprehensive analysis of quantification in Slavic, see Kosta (2008). Our claims here will be much more programmatic, so we refer the reader to Kosta's work for details.

"All Italians are loud, but I know one that is not"

There seems to be no *logical contradiction* here, but rather the refutation of an inductive generalization. Therefore, the sentence is not only intelligible but also interpretable by the semantic component. There is a relevant contrast, however, clear in examples like (60):

(60) # Cada (uno de los) italianos es gritón,
pero conozco a uno que no lo es
Each of the Italians is loud, but I know one is not.

This situation can be formally represented as follows, to clarify the procedural instruction conveyed by quantifiers and its compatibility with a clause that cancel the implicature:

(61) Engl. *Every* / Germ. *Alle* = $\forall(x) / \forall(\exists(x))$
Cada = $\forall (\exists(x))$
Todo = $\forall(x)$

Once we have clarified the procedural instructions of these quantifiers, we are able to go back to the examples. The sentence in (59) is acceptable because a *generic* statement is not incompatible with an exceptional case, and the adversative clause does not create ungrammaticality. The statement is valid for the whole class *perfectively*, and therefore a clause in which *specific members* of the aforementioned class do not belong to the extension of the main predicate is licensed, since the internal complexity of the set is of no interest. We will call "Todo" [*all*] a *weak universal quantifier*. In the case of "cada" [*each*], we will propose that the universal quantifier has in turn scope over an existential quantifier, so that the cancellation of the implicature is impossible:. We will call "cada" [each] a strong universal quantifier. Note that, although both quantifiers can appear on coordination structures, the order is determined by a weak-strong dynamic:

(62) Todos [all] y cada uno [each] de los ...
Cada uno y todos los...

If we have made a strong statement (i.e., a statement containing a strong Q) is because we have propositions in our mental context that license such a move. It is semantically anomalous to immediately weaken the quantifier, however, the reverse movement is perfectly acceptable and natural:

(63) Todos, es más, cada uno de los...
All, what is more, each of the...

These coordination structures such as (62) should be interpreted in fact as (63), in which there is added emphasis and a strengthening of the statement, with the additional benefit of generating more positive cognitive effects, therefore making the structure more relevant in the technical sense.

In summary, the formulation of the explicit (procedural) semantics of quantifiers proposed by Russell does not work for natural languages (and it is questionable whether such a characterization is useful for formal languages) since, for example, it is not able to cover crosslinguistic differences properly and inferential properties.

7. Appendix 2
Remarks on Categorization: Syntax "all-the-way-down"

Proposal: *Categorization of roots depends on Merge and is, therefore, interface-driven and interface-recognized.*

Weak Proposal: Roots have a *categorial potentiality*, which, *in abstracto*, comprises all possible outcomes (i.e., categorial perspectives to be read off at the semantic interface) The outcome depends on the semantic instructions of the procedural element (*Time, Determiner* and *Preposition*). *Merge is possible because √ and X share ontological format* (Boeckx, 2010a; Krivochen, 2011a)

Why is that the case? Both roots and procedural nodes convey (interpretable, if the note is needed) semantic information. As "bundles" of dimensions, they have the same ontology. The conceptual / procedural character is determined *in the interpretative interface*, it is of no relevance to syntax, which is purely generative. Free combination is thus possible. Any other option has to be *explained and justified* in principled terms.

Our hypothesis is that *there is no distinction between "categorial / sub-categorial levels"* (Cf. Panagiotidis, 2010), this is, word-level / morphemic-level affecting operations. Derivations are built by *free unbounded Merge* according to *ontological format* (monotonic Merge) and *structural format* (Generalized Transformations), only restricted by interface conditions, outside syntax itself. "Lexical derivations" (i.e., the mechanisms of word formation) are in no way different to "syntactic derivations", thus, there is no conceptual reason to posit two different levels of representation or conditions on well-formedness.

A direct consequence of the aforementioned hypothesis is that "lexical decomposition" in the syntax is simply unformulable. The syntax proper receives fully-fledged complex conceptual structures instantiated as roots (see below). Any "decomposition" study is plausible at the *conceptual* level, not at the *lexical* level.

Let us analyze a sample derivation, following the framework outlined so far.

Sample derivation:

Roots enter the working area "uncategorized", in their (pre-categorial) ψ-state. The *Conservation Principle* on the one hand and *interface conditions* on the other constrain possible combinations, as the information conveyed by the RSS must be maintained, and that tells us what the clausal skeleton could look like; and semantic interface conditions filter trivial merges (like {{a}} -see Adger, 2011- or the previously mentioned {α, ∅}) and other "ill formednesses" ({D, P} and so on) *post-syntactically* (*restrictivist theory*). Categorization patterns will be analyzed later on.

Syntax proceeds in a strict bottom-up fashion, Merge applying to elements sharing ontological format (e.g., D and v) or structural format (e.g., in traditional terms, "non-terminals". So-called "specifiers", for example, would merge this way). The primacy of monotonic Merge and the deletion of the categorial / sub-categorial distinction (which presupposes two levels of syntactic computation, i.e., two derivational spaces) give us a **unified syntactic model *"all-the-way-down"*** (Phoevos Panagiotidis, p.c.)

Here we have a resultant ditransitive Logical Form (in Relevance Theory terms), with "labels" *recognized* for explicature purposes only:

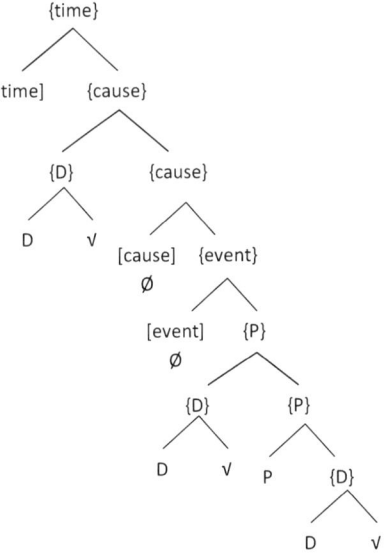

Notes:
i) [] indicate semantic primitives, whereas {} indicate *recognized labels* at the C-I interface, where they are relevant to build an explicature as labeling entails scope. This means that a Radically Bare Phrase Structure could dispense with {}, but not with [] notation.
ii) The *event* and *cause* nodes are always *phonologically empty* (i.e., p-defective, see Hale & Keyser, 2002). This means that **there are no verbs as primitive categories**.
iii) √ are roots, *pre*-categorial linguistic instantiations of *a*-categorial (and severely underspecified) C-I generic concepts, following the *Conservation Principle*. The incorporation processes Mateu proposes are not likely to happen "in real (derivational) time", but *historically*, as they have to do with the insertion of a *coined* phonological piece Spelling Out, for example, [manner] + [motion]. Thus, "fly", for example, is taken as a simple root in both: [Birds fly] (simple Unergative construction) and [I have to fly home] (Path of Motion construction: "manner incorporation"). Compositionality does the rest of the work when building an explicature in C-I.

Our hypothesis is the following: Roots do not have dimensions whatsoever. Configuration is enough for C-I_2 to determine the "perspective" to be taken over the semantic substance. Local relation [X...√] is enough to create "categorial interpretations" of roots, there is no need to posit quantum categorial dimensions. This depends on the relation *procedural category – perspective on the root* being one-to-one, as it seems.

That said, *nominalizations* (which have proven quite conflictive since Chomsky, 1970) result from *eventive* (either *caused* or *uncaused*) RSS, instantiated in the syntax and merged with [D]. √ can be "light" or "heavy", which determines Spell Out, as in verbal structures. Of course, {event} must appear, because of the *Conservation Principle*. The appearance of {cause} will depend on whether the semantic construal is *caused* (unergative, -di-transitive) or not (unaccusative).

RSS:
Unaccusative RSS   Possible syntactic realizations:

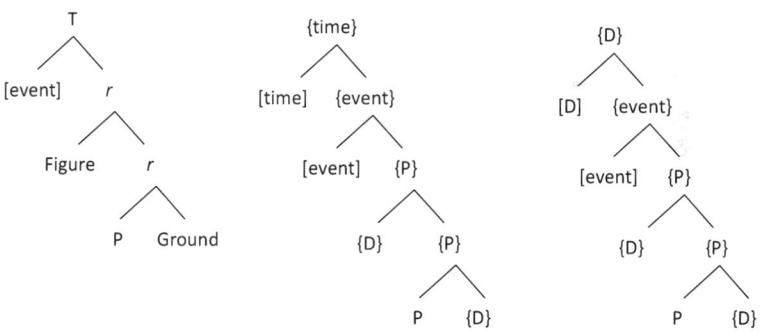

e.g.: [$_T$ arrive [$_r$ Mary [$_r$ AT] the house]]   Mary arrived (at the house)   Mary's arrival (at the house)

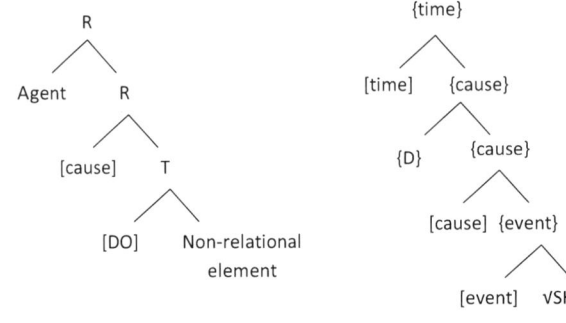

e.g.: [R Mary [R cause [T [T DO] shout]]]　　Mary shouted　　Mary´s shout

- [D...α...√] = N, being α an X number of procedural nodes that do not collapse categorial dimensions on the root, because they are not categorically specified enough (that is, they can appear in both N and V structures, see above for examples of how both [cause] and [event] are underspecified in this way). No immediate adjacency is needed, we just have to respect Minimality. D is specified enough as regards content and distribution to determine interpretation, and the same happens with the other PPCC. The key is on the *rigidity of procedural meaning*: root meaning, for it is underspecified semantically, is malleable. Procedural elements are not, as they provide instructions as to how to manipulate the roots.

- [T...α...√] = V

- [P...α... √] = A, Adv (Hale & Keyser, Mateu)

> ***Therefore***: *all we need is √ and procedural categories (closed system), free combination and interface conditions take care of everything else.*

Chapter 3: Empirical problems
0 Introduction

This chapter is devoted to the analysis of problematic phenomena concerning NC in several languages, Germanic, Slavic and Romance. The objective is to verify to what extent Radical Minimalism is capable of providing simple and elegant explanations following the basic desideratum of eliminating intra-syntactical conditions and providing third-factor non-stipulative accounts. To this end, we will focus our attention on *possessive* and *partitive* constructions, *relational adjectives* and *intra-NC clitic climbing*. We will not make reference to previous proposals unless absolutely necessary, as we leave the comparison task to the reader.

1.1 Possessor Raising and Partitive Readings

In this section we will analyze two structures that have been object of different lines of analysis, *possessor raising* within the nominal construction on the one hand and *double predication* on the other. Our goal is to present a unified account of both, under Radically Minimalist assumptions.

German is an example of a language that allows so-called *possessor raising*. Most accounts (e.g., Grohmann, 2003 for a recent point of view) assume a derivational relation between *genitive possessive* structures and *possessor raising*, giving the following pairs (taken from Grohmann, 2003: 203):

(1) German:
    a)   Annas Wagen
           Anna$_{GEN}$ car
    b)   Der Anna ihr Wagen
           Anna$_{DEF}$ her car

Derivational accounts assume Movement to a functional node between D and N, *á la* Cinque (1999) and the FP hypothesis. The main problem is how to justify that movement taking place in the syntax without adding superfluous elements to the representation (e.g., an OCC/EPP/EF feature).

In consonance with the *token-Merge theory of movement* in Chapter 1, we will argue that there is no Movement in the "displacement" interpretation, but re-Merge of a *token* in a Top-like position in order to generate a *contrastive interpretation* at the C-I interface (i.e., interface-driven Merge), as it occurs with clitic doubling and PP fronting. The highest *visible* (i.e., Spelled-Out) node is D, and it is spelled-out only once as this is *enough* to generate drastic interface effects (i.e., contrastive value). In more general terms, possession is an *unaccusative* relation between a Figure (the possessed object) and a Ground (the possessor), related by a *central coincidence* preposition. We are not constrained by labeling in the syntax, so the tree would look like as follows:

(2)

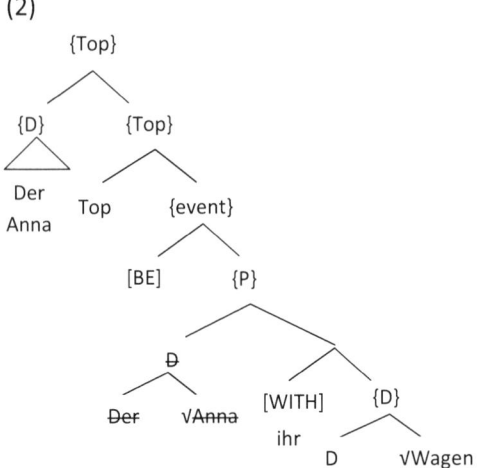

The Genitive version (a) is the result of P-onto-D incorporation within the locative structure: bear in mind that, as we have already claimed in Krivochen (2010c), Genitive case belongs within the Dative sphere, that is, it is an inferential refinement of a more general (central coincidence) Locative relation.

The verb *have*, the phonological manifestation of the {event} node in the structure above, is an *atelic* event with a *central coincidence relation*, and that is why we have represented possession as a prepositional phrase. Moreover, the alternance [TO] / [WITH] has already been posited for PIOC / DOC alternations, in which the DOC generates a drastic C-I effect: a *presupposition* of the *possession* of the theme:

(3)
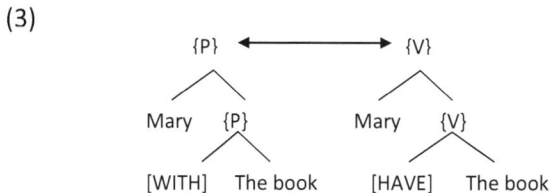

The very same representation we have used in (2), however, is valid for superficially different structures, present in other languages. The *contrastive value* is maintained, but the Spell-Out of another D token generates an aditional *partitive reading* which justifies the extra-effort for the SM-interface, in consonance with Kosta & Krivochen (in preparation)'s *Anti-Spell-Out* desideratum which we repeat here for the reader's comfort:

(4) *Anti Spell-Out generalization*

Spell-Out as few elements as needed for convergence, unless there is a powerful interface reason to Spell-Out elements that are **not** strictly necessary for plain convergence.

The relevant structures are like the following:

(5) Ancient Greek (omitting spirits and accents):
 a) Οι αγθοι ππoι
     The good horses
 b) Οι ιπποι οι αγθοι
     The horses the good [ones]

And the corresponding tree-like representation, which is the very same as in (2):

(6)
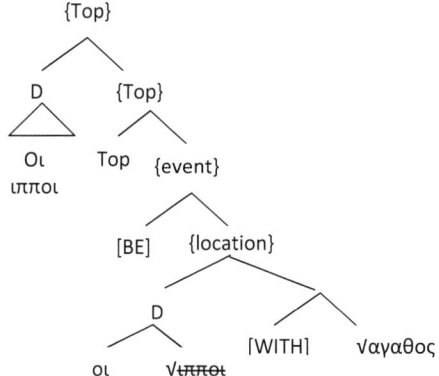

Even though the Spell Out of the D [οι] is necessary for the partitive reading (as in English "The best ∅ of the students", with the only change that it is the lower root that is Spelled Out), the root can occur only once and no meaning is lost, therefore, only the D is materialized. In an interface-driven system, which looks for optimal relevance (i.e., relation cost-benefit) in every operation, this is not only possible but also desirable. The category adjective for [αγαθος] is interface-recognized from the local relation [P...√], as we have already claimed in Krivochen (2011d). The part-whole relation requires two determiners (one for the part, another for the whole?), whereas so-called "possessor raising" does not, just Token-Merge in a Top-like position to generate contrastive implicatures.

1.2 *Possessor* rising and *possessed* thematization

The German structures we presented in the previous section configure an interesting paradigm, namely:

(7)   a.   Mein Freund
My friend
      b.   Der Freund meiner Schwester
The$_{GEN}$ friend my sister$_{GEN}$
      c.   Meiner Schwester ihr Freund (= (1))
My sister$_{GEN}$ her friend

Interestingly, German does not allow a literal equivalent of the sentence in (8):

(8)   My sister's friend

German allows two options: either [Meiner Schwester], the *possessor*, is token-merged in Top, as we have done above (for example (c)), or [Der Freund], the *possessed* entity, is positioned in a *theme*-related position since there is no contrastive value in (b)[37] and therefore it would be inaccurate to consider that there is a token in a Top-like position. English, on the other hand, presents a different picture: unless explicitly signaled by intonation, there is no contrastive value in (8), and it is the *possessor* that is merged in a theme-related position. The English structure we propose goes along the lines of (9), to be contrasted with (2):

---

37   The difference between (a) and (b) resides on the implicatures they generate. To say of a person that he/she is "Mein Freund" is interpreted as "boyfriend / girlfriend", whereas (b) is neutral at this respect.

(9)

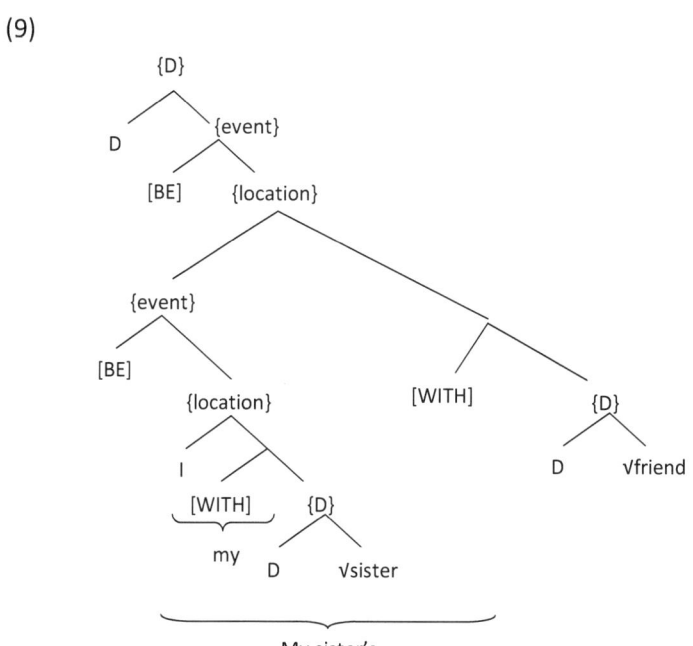

This structure reinforces our conception of possession as abstract central coincidence location, while all categorial correlations as explained in Chapter 1 are respected. Both [sister] and [friend] are definite referential arguments, therefore, they must be {D, √} structures. The whole locative complex, however, is in itself a referential argument, therefore, the presence of {D} on the top is expected. Moreover, Radically Minimalist Minimality (see Chapter 2 and below) allows us to reinforce the definiteness of [my], since there is no distributionally restricted procedural node between ["I"] and [D]. Now, what about the *theme-related* position we mentioned above? We have already showed that, within the clausal domain, the external position licensed by T is related to *themehood*, but: is there such a position within the NC? We believe so. Our hypothesis is the following: the *theme*-related position within the NC is licensed by the locative node, in the position where Figures are conceptually interpreted (in traditional terms, Spec-P, but we are not constrained by 2-D tree-like syntax, which we use *only* for expository purposes). [My sister] has no contrastive value because its syntactic position does not convey such a semantic effect.

A further note about possession is in order here: is English ['s] a *clitic* (as Radeva-Bork, 2012 claims) or a *case mark*? Abney (1987) supports the idea it is a CL in D₀ raising to Spec-DP, but we find at least two arguments against such a proposal:
- It is not an argument, rather, a *locative* predicate
- It only appears within full DP nominals but crucially *not* with pronouns, which inflect for Case:
  i. A friend of [$_{DP}$ John's]
  ii. A friend of mine
  iii. *A friend of [$_{DP}$ [$_D$ mine's] √THING]] (see Panagiotidis, 2002 for an analysis of pronouns as D with empty root complements)

A fundamental distinction must be done: the phonological exponent of a given node (be it conceptual or procedural) does not provide at all a clear path to understanding its syntax, and even less so, its semantics. Consider the well-known and influential Y-model, traceable to the Standard Theory (see particularly Chomsky, 1965), but used, although many times implicitly, in other theories of functional roots:

(10)

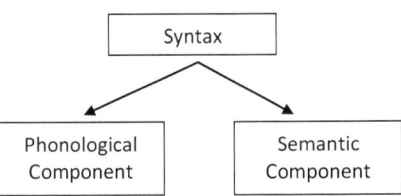

Research within generative grammar (and other models, like SFL) has taken the PC-S path, which means inducing syntax from phonology (e.g., Kayne, 1994 and subsequent work). Of course, this methodological choice has lead to progress within the descriptive field, as Koster (2010) points out, but little progress regarding explanation has been made, because semantic structure has most frequently been wiped under the rug. Radical Minimalism goes the other way around, asking "which syntactic structure could, assuming the simplest mapping, result in X semantic interpretation?" Even if the structures we propose seem *prima facie* more complex than orthodox theories (e.g., Abney's 1987, see section 4. below), it seems clear to us that those allegedly more economic proposals cannot account for a number of semantic effects that are by no means part of the "peripheral grammar", but of its very core.

2 Clitic Climbing within the Bulgarian {D}[38]

The framework outlined so far also accounts for intra-{D} clitic climbing. Let us consider the following Bulgarian examples (taken from Kosta & Zimmerling, 2011):

(11) stolicata   ni   //   [*stolica ni]
     $capital_{DEF}$ our_{DAT}
     'our capital'.
     mladata   ni   stolica //   [*mlada ni stolica]
     $young_{DEF}$ our_{DAT} capital
     'our young capital'.
     večno   mladata   ni   stolica
     eternally $young_{DEF}$ our_{DAT} capital
     'our eternally young capital'
     [*večno mlada ni stolica]

Kosta & Zimmerling, building on a suggestion from Krivochen (p.c.), analyze the data above proposing that the relation between definiteness and possession is semantically reinforced by the fact that one cannot [have] (a central coincidence prepositional relation, [WITH]) a "generic" thing. Furthermore, they claim that the relation between the adjective and the definite article adjoined to it, "jumping over" the possessive is licensed by a feature-defined version of Rizzi's (1990) Relativized Minimality:

(12) *Feature-defined Minimality Principle*

A head $X^0 = \{F_1, F_2...F_n\}$ and a head $Z^0 = \{F_1, F_2...F_n\}$ *can relate by any syntactic process with respect to a feature F_x from their feature bundle iff there is no Y^0 between X and Z* **that has F_x in its feature bundle**. *Otherwise, Y^0 is invisible for the effect of computational operations.*

The structure would be as follows:

(13) [XP [$X_{[F1, F2]}$] [YP [$Y_{[F1]}$] [ZP [$Z_{[F1, F2]}$]]]]

If the relation between X and Z depends on [F2], then the Y head is invisible for probing purposes, and that is essential for their argumentation. However, appealing though that proposal might be, it has a fundamental problem: it depends on *feature valuation / checking mechanisms*, which we have dispensed with in Radical Minimalism. We reformulate *Minimali-*

---

38   For a thorough *description* of the distribution of Bulgarian clitics, see Radeva-Bork (2012) and references therein. Examples were checked with native speakers.

ty not in terms of *features* but in terms of *intervenient tokens*, obtaining what we call *Radically Minimalist Minimality*:

(14) Radically Minimalist Minimality (RMM)

A node X = {$D_1, D_2...D_n$} and a node Z = {$D_1, D_2...D_n$} can be related at the interface I iff:
a) there is no Y structurally between X and Z that has a procedural instruction that can generate a drastic interface effect in X.
b) there is no Y structurally between X and Z such that Y is a token of either X or Z
Otherwise, Y is invisible for the purpose of interface effects.

The relation *at the interface* (not in the syntax, since it is only a generative algorithm) we are talking about is, in this case, with respect to a dimension D, but it does not necessarily be limited to that (it works, for example, for Chain Reduction purposes, see Krivochen & Kosta, in preparation).

Now, we are in conditions to reanalyze the data presented above. The question "How does the clitic [-ta] jump over the Poss onto Adj?" does not arise in our model. The representation would be as follows, in line with Krivochen (2011e), and taking into account the categorial correlations in Chapter 1:

(15) Bg mlad*a*ta ni stolica // [*mlada ni stolica]
young$_{Def}$ our$_{Dat}$ capital
'our young capital'.

(16)

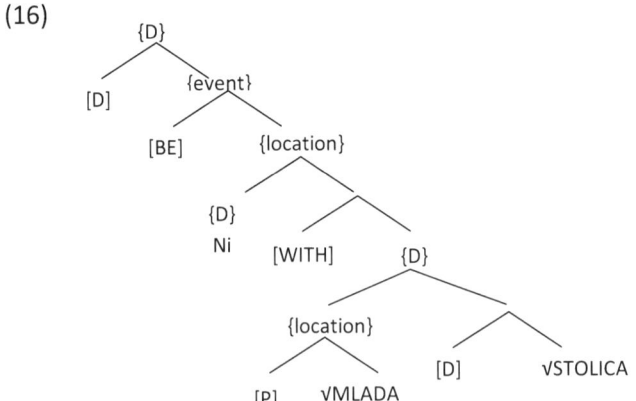

We will work under the assumption that there are *two kinds of clitics*, from a phonological point of view: strong and weak. Strong clitics are those that attract a host, whereas a weak clitic adjoins a host rather than attracting it, thus appearing in different places in the final linearized phonological form. In this case, what we have in the syntactic structure is an *atelic static* event, and a *spatial relation*, which accounts for the possessive relation: the [BE]-[WITH] combination is semantically interpreted as the primitive verb [HAVE], which is, all in all, what is finally interpreted at the explicature level. [stolica] is semantically interpreted as N because its nearest procedural element is [D], and [mlada] is semantically interpreted as A because its nearest procedural element is [P]. [D] has a definiteness dimension, which is interpreted because of the simple fact that, if we have a possessor, we must have a *non-generic / indefinite* thing possessed. It is not, therefore, a "feature" within D, as in orthodox minimalist works, but rather the result of an inferential process that, assuming – our biologically oriented version of – RT as a plausible theory for the C-I interface, does not increase the computational cost and simplifies the system by making it more componential. Back to the initial question, we will remind the reader of our *Morpheme Formation Constraint* (see Krivochen, 2011a, d, e, Kosta & Krivochen, 2012):

(17) **Morpheme formation constraint**: *We cannot group features in a terminal node (i.e., morpheme) if there is no vocabulary item in the B List specified enough to be inserted in that node.*

If Bulgarian does not admit the [Def] componential element to be Spelled Out in N (Radeva-Bork, p.c.), it searches the closest element in the surrounding space, what we have called "energy levels" in our 3-D syntactic model (i.e., within a *local* domain in 2-D terms), as in our *atomic structure theory* (Krivochen, 2011e, 2012b).

Let us assume that {P} (= A) is in the immediate next "energy level". The adjoining of the [Def] affix to {P} is natural, in our model, as it follows from interface conditions (MFC) and architectural features of symbolic structures in a quantum mind. The element is present in the syntax, as there is nothing in the inference that is not licensed by a procedural node, interpretable at C-I. The MFC, as it is obvious, affects the "road to PF", correspondingly, it has no access to semantic information. Semantic componentiality and phonological synthesis are thus unrelated processes, as it should be clear from the architecture outlined in Chapter 1.

3 Spanish Relational Adjectives[39]

We have already made it clear that As are not a basic category, like in Hale & Keyser's (1993) framework but arise at the interface as the interpretation of the local relation between {P} and a root. We will follow Fábregas (forthcoming) in defining *relational adjectives* as **denoting arguments of the noun that they modify, the latter without being necessarily "deverbal"**[40]. We will revisit the data presented there and offer an alternative derivation for these structures. Let us work on some examples, which we take to belong to different sub-groups of relational adjectives, each with a subjacent RSS and consequently different syntactic structure. This gives rise to differences in interpretation at the *explicature* level, which we will analyze below (some are taken from Fábregas, forthcoming):

a) La invasión *italiana* de Albania [the *Italian* invasion of Albania]; La pesca *ballenera japonesa* [The *japanese whale$_{REL}$ fish*]; La producción *lechera* [The *milk$_{REL}$* production]; El bombardeo *estadounidense* [The *US-american* bombarding]

b) Un dolor *muscular* [A *muscular* pain]; Un problema *legal* [A *legal* problem]; Un juicio *político* [A *political* trial]

c) Un viaje *estelar* [A *star$_{REL}$* trip]; El calentamiento *global* [The *global* warming]; La contaminación *sonora* The *sound$_{REL}$* pollution]

We will now analyze each group in turn.

3.1 Group (a)

This group corresponds roughly to Bosque's (1991) *Thematic adjectives*, even though we will try to justify our proposal of a separate group before giving it a name. In this case, we have a *caused eventive* RSS, which is instantiated in the syntax from {cause} to the bottom and merged with D, determining the categorial interpretation of the closest root. Let us analyze an example:

(18) "La invasión *italiana* de Albania"

---

39 This section is mostly based on Krivochen (2011f), published in "Sorda y Sonora", Revista del Instituto de Lingüística, PUCP.

40 Of course, in a category-less *syntax* as the one we posit, it makes no sense talking about "*deverbal* nouns".

For this, we propose a *locatum* structure, analogous to that of [break]. Regardless of the nature of the *r* node (which is never fixed beforehand, but depends on the non-relational elements that occupy the positions of "figure" and "ground": we could very well have had a *location* structure), we have a *caused event* including a *relational node*, so this is the most complex RSS we can find. Our interest now is how we instantiate this in the syntax without losing information, and making sure that each root is under the scope of a suitable procedural head for categorial interpretation purposes. Our proposal at this respect is the following, which we take to be valid for any relational adjective of group (a):

(19)

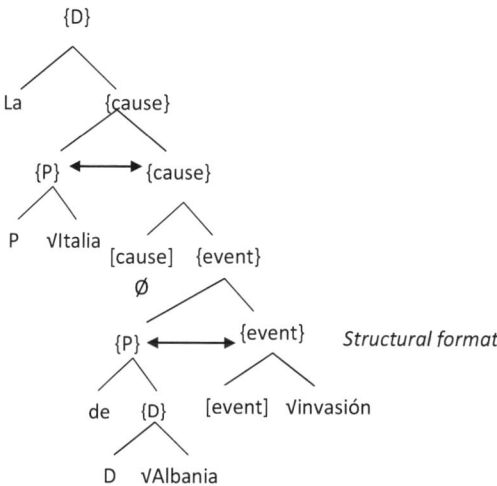

Structural format

Here we have all the information conveyed by the RSS, plus procedural elements whose distribution is specified enough so that they create categorial interpretations in the LF interface level and thus allow for a fully-fledged explicature to be built.

3.2 Group (b)

In this second group we have adjectives whose underlying RSS is *uncaused*, so there is no {cause} primitive in the syntax and therefore no initiator. We will take the *r* node to be *terminal*, and this is an interesting generalization should it be proven true: the A denotes a characteristic that is not inherent to the N, but determines a *subset* of the class denoted by the N: of all problems, the *legal* ones. The A categorial interpretation is instantiated in the syntax as a {P, √} construction, following our earlier claim. The transitional eventive node is *stative*, as there is no change of state: the structure would be parallel to *unaccusative attributive constructions*, and we will only find *stage level predicates*, according to our generalization. Let us see an example:

"Un dolor *muscular*"

The syntactic instantiation would be as follows:

(20)

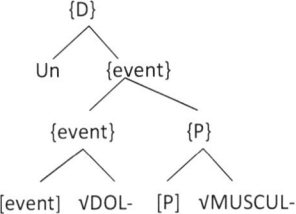

The considerations regarding {P} are the same as in group (a), there is Merge by *structural format*, and no influence of P over √DOL-. Notice that, even though the trees should be label-less, the *bare structure* resembles that of Restrictive Relative Clauses, traditionally said to be CPs adjunct to NP. We can think of relational adjectives in Spanish (always post-nominal) as *abridged restrictive relative clauses*, since the structure licenses that interpretation.

The same happens with "Un problema *legal*". We follow Chomsky's (2009) claim that headedness is an epiphenomenon in the syntax, and we have gone further by explaining where and why does headedness play a role (see Krivochen, 2011a, c). In these cases, notice that what we want to say is that there is a special kind of problem, or that the pain is located in a certain part of our body. The conceptual "heads" of those constructions are, then, *problem* and *pain* ("problema" and "dolor"). That is why both generic concepts are *figures* in their respective Relational Semantic Structures (RSS), and the *ground* denotes a location, either physical (a body part) or metaphorical (a certain domain, like law). The RSS of "Un problema *legal*" would be:

(21)   [T [BE] [r problema [r [AT] ley]]]

There is, we can see, a certain *existential* flavor: there exists a problem in a certain domain, there is a pain in a certain part of the body. This is licensed in the semantic interface by the presence of the *stative eventive node* BE, and the fact reinforces our thesis that there is *unaccusativity* at the very core of the semantics of A.

3.3 Group (c)

The adjectives in this group share much with those in group (b), but there are some fundamental differences that justify the division of two categories. Both classes include *uncaused* RSSs and have a *terminal coincidence* relational node. However, the *eventive node* is *dynamic*, i.e., [GO], therefore, we are dealing with structures that convey a change of location, provided that states are abstract locations. Besides, the spell-out of the N head depends on an incorporated root (Acedo-Matellán, 2010), so we are dealing with *manner incorporation*, a structure analogous to a *Path of Motion* construction. Let us analyze an example:

(22) "Un viaje *estelar*"

RSS:

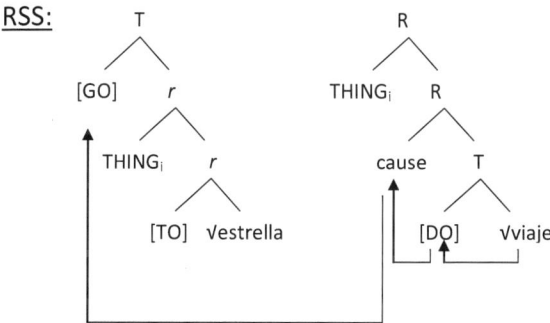

The incorporated root instantiates an *unergative* construal, and the goal structure is an *unaccusative* one (thus resembling a Path of Motion construction). However, the syntactic instantiation takes the fully-fledged pre-categorial root as a whole, as all the information is conveyed by that root. There is no overt initiator in the final structure, as the instantiation of THING as √THING and its correspondent Spell-Out would be completely irrelevant (see Krivochen, 2011c for a similar argument regarding demonstratives). However, the initiator must be present in the syntactic structure so as not to violate the *Conservation Principle*. We assume that the initiator of the *unergative* construal is the same that undergoes the change of location in the *unaccusative* structure, and that allows us to link both construals. The [cause] primitive in the unergative construal must be instantiated in the syntax, following the Conservation Principle. The resulting structure is as follows:

(23)

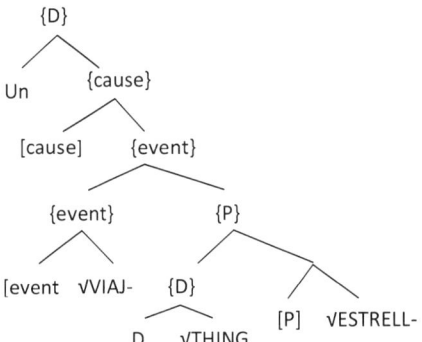

Both roots √VIAJ- and √ESTRELL- are, once under the scope of a procedural head, semantically specified enough to receive interpretation in the explicature level. √THING, on the other hand, is not. Even under the scope of a [D] procedural head (without which the derivation would collapse in the interface level), the root is not specified enough to be worth spelling out, as every overt element adds computational cost and that bargain must be balanced by a raise in the positive cognitive effects extracted.

The second example is different, as there is no *manner incorporation*, but there is change of state. The affected constituent is overtly realized in the form of the adjective: in "el calentamiento *global*", it is the "globe" that "heats". The corresponding structures would be:

(24)

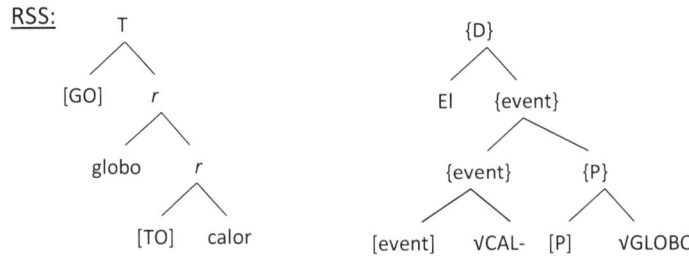

The last example seems very different, but it is analyzable in the same terms, the only thing being that we are dealing with an *unergative* construal in which the Agent is realized as the relational adjective:

(25) [R sonido [R [*cause*] [T [DO] contaminación]]]

Given the differences between those structures, the reader may be asking himself why we put both examples in the same category. The answer is that *manner incorporation* is just a coining procedure, what is really important is the root that is instantiated in the syntax and the meaning conveyed by the eventive node, whether it is *positive* (DO, GO) or *negative* (BE). The nature of the semi-transitional eventive node T is, in our opinion, a decisive fact in the classification of these structures, since it determines interpretation to a great extent, and is present in every structure we have seen so far. The *cause* variable is put in a second place when determining the sub-type of the A, as the relevant information is codified from {event} / T down.

4 Possessives as Locations and the Italian {D}

The syntax of possessives has been the object of several analyses. Pre-DP hypotheses put them as NPs appearing as NP specifiers (and even N'''), like in Jackendoff's (1977) proposal. In Abney's terms, possessives are generated as D heads, then incorporated onto the DP-Spec:

(26)

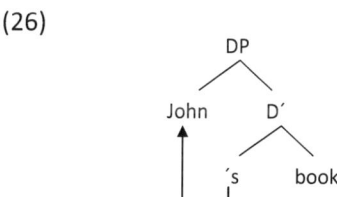

We find the same failure in both proposals: they consider that possessives (both affixal of full XPs) are nominal in nature. On the contrary, we will propose that possessive structures are actually *prepositional*, on the line of what we (following Miechowicz-Mathiasen) have proposed for numerals. Moreover, we will make a strong prediction regarding the *nature* of the locative procedural node: it is a *central coincidence* relational element. Our case will be based on the possessives within the Italian DP[41]. Let us see some examples:

(27) La casa
The house
(28) La mia casa
The my house

A structure like (27) has an exact Spanish parallel, but (28) is plainly impossible. In Spanish, the co-occurrence of an overt definite determiner and a possessive is only marginally accepted and in a very restricted set of contexts, like humoristic expressions:

(29) "Este triunfo le canto con alegría / porque me quiere tanto *la yegua mía* (Les Luthiers, "La Yegua Mía", *Recital 74*, 1974)

Italian also allows the insertion of an adjective, whose locative nature has been widely acknowledged (see Jackendoff, 1983; Mateu, 2000). However, not all adjectives are equally acceptable: there is a strong preference for *individual level predicates* (ILP) over *stage level predicates* (SLP):

(30) La mia figlia piccola
The my daughter little$_{FemSg}$

With *stage level predicates*, acceptability drastically decreases in pure attributive position:

(31) #La mia figlia stanca
The my daughter tired$_{FemSg}$

(31) is only very marginally acceptable, either if the predicate is interpreted inferentially as ILP (this is, change the nature of the locative relation) or if the context is, as in the Spanish example, humoristic. Acceptability with the pure SLP reading can be improved by the addition of an overt [BE], or a heavier predicate, like [sentire] (*to feel*) or [pensare] (*to think*):

(32) La mia figlia piccola si sente stanca
The my daughter small CL$_{REFL}$ feel$_{3SgPresImpf}$ tired$_{FemSg}$

We claim that this decrease of acceptability is due to the fact that the two predications within the nominal construction should coincide in nature in order to achieve optimal relevance, minimizing parsing cost. Of course,

---

41 We are grateful to Erica Corbara for providing both the Italian examples and acceptability judgements.

since the operations in the syntactic component are driven by DFI, that is, by interface needs, there is no "ungrammaticality" in the sense of "syntactic ill-formedness". We have to account for the difference via interface conditions in order to derive the tendency in a non-stipulative way. Our claim is the following: given the fact that ILP are preferred over SLP, the locative semantic primitive involved in possession is the same as in ILP. The suggested fully developed structure for (30) is as follows:

(33)

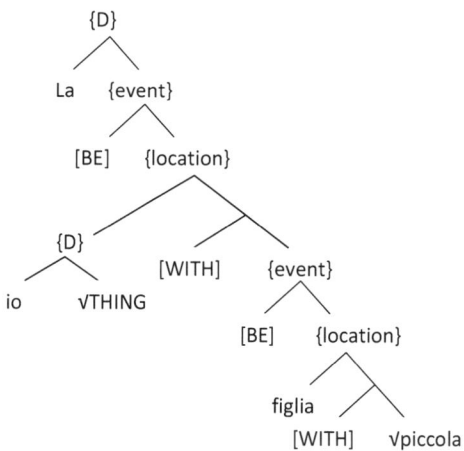

We see that within the nominal domain there are only central coincidence locative nodes, an identity that, expectedly, makes semantic parsing much easier than when locative predicates of different nature co-occur (i.e., central-terminal). If the semantic pre-linguistic structure (i.e., RSS) can be instantiated via a minimal number of procedural *types*[42], it should be. In other words: *"do not use more elements than you strictly need"*. This is, of course, a consideration out of third-factor principles, particularly *principles of efficient computation*. The change in the degree of acceptability with SLP stems from the fact that SLP, which denote transitory states, include a *terminal coincidence* locative node within their semantic structure, and the identity preference is not met.

---

42 [WITH] and [TO] are procedural *types*, each instantiation within a linguistic structure would count as a *token*. Multiplying the tokens does not violate Occam's Razor as far as that multiplication is interface-justified, but multiplication of *types* beyond interface requirements leads to severe computational overload.

Regarding categorial interpretations, we see that each minimal domain is built respecting *Radically Minimalist Minimality*: the local relation between [WITH] and [√piccola] results in the A [piccola]. [Figlia] is interpreted as a sortal entity because the pronoun [io] is already interpreted as a fully fledged {D} structure in which there is a generic root whose Spell-Out is irrelevant (in the technical sense), just like in demonstratives (see Chapter 2).

5 A note on affixes

In this section we will discuss a possibility that has been suggested by De Belder (2011), namely, *affixes are roots*, and not functional / procedural elements, as we claim. We will give some theoretical evidence in favor of her hypothesis, and then justify our contrary position, so that the reader can decide between both options.

De Belder's claim is that affixes can have many different meanings and some of them stretch "well beyond functional meaning" (De Belder, p.c.). In this sense, they allegedly share characteristics with conceptual categories rather than with procedural categories, since only the former are "malleable" (Escandell Vidal & Leonetti, 2011: 4):

> "(...) In the cognitive pragmatic tradition, it is common to assume that conceptual representations are flexible and malleable, which means that they can be enriched, elaborated on and adjusted in different ways to meet the expectations of relevance. All the interpretive phenomena that are usually considered as instances of meaning modulation and ad hoc concept formation stem from this basic property (Wilson 2003, Wilson and Carston 2007). We claim that instructions, on the contrary, are rigid[43]: they cannot enter into the mutual adjustment processes, nor can they be modulated to comply with the requirements of conceptual representations, either linguistically communicated or not. (...)"[44]

In our (2011c) paper we identified conceptual categories with *roots* since, as they are semantically underspecified, their interpretation is shaped by the procedural categories that have scope over them. If affixes are as malleable as De Belder claims, then they *must* be roots, and Escandell & Leo-

---

43   Note the parallel with early DM (Noyer, 1998): f-morphemes' Spell-Out was said to be "deterministic", whereas l-morphemes' Spell-Out was free.
44   Procedural instructions, for example, force the semantic component to adopt *ad hoc* propositions to understand an utterance. See Escandell Vidal & Leonetti (2011: 7).

netti's quote supports her view. However, there are some problems with this proposal:
- If affixes are roots, and therefore malleable, which node provides the procedural instructions that narrow possible interpretations?
- Root Terminal Nodes (RTN) cannot be merged to one another as they are empty sets, so *ad hoc* functional FPs are posited thus violating, to our understanding, Dynamic Full Interpretation: {∅} and {F, {∅}} are equally legible (if ∅ is legible at all, which is not clear to us as it provides no information for explicature building or for any other purposes, if it is really "radically empty").

In our proposal, affixes are *procedural nodes*, thus, they *cannot* be roots. The main reason is that they provide C-I with instructions as to how to interpret the generic content of a root, which is there from the very beginning of the derivational path (because of the Conservation Principle). Prefixes are Ps and suffixes tend to Spell-Out {event} / {cause}, both of which have scope over the root, and thus *categorial interpretations* are licensed. Notice that, if prefixes are Ps, we are adopting a version of the *locative theory*, which claims that conceptualization is essentially and primarily *spatial*. We see that procedural instructions like Polarity and Aspect can be expressed ultimately in locative terms, as well as fine Aktionsart distinctions, which is a desirable consequence as the system is substantially simplified. Of course, some fine-grade flavors are inferential, but we have seen in previous works (mainly, Krivochen, 2010a) that inference is pre-sub-determined by the syntactic configuration: there is nothing in the inference that is not there in the syntax (because information cannot be created or destroyed, just transformed, as it is ultimately *energy*), but the inferential component can re-parse an LF (in Relevance Theoretic terms) if the first and more accessible option does not fulfill the Relevance expectations. The debate is now set, in whole new terms.

We take *all Romance/Germanic prefixes to be spelled-out Ps*, as there is always a *locative* meaning involved, which establishes how the root is to be interpreted. Extending the hypothesis, affixes in general are *procedural nodes*, functional terminals that have scope over roots' underspecified generic semantic content. Even *polarity* prefixes (dis-, un-), and *aspectual* prefixes can be taken to be Ps, despite their highly abstract meaning[45]:

---

45 In these terms, *perfectivity* would be related to *central coincidence*, whereas *imperfectivity* would be related to *terminal coincidence*. This provisional hypo-

Dis- = [$_{Path}$ OUT OF [$_{Place}$ WITH]]
En- (inchoative aspect) = [$_{Path}$ TO [$_{Place}$ WITH]]

And some other examples:

Aspect: re- (Latin / Spanish) iterative
-σκ- (Greek) iterative
en/m- (Spanish) inchoative
in- (Latin) inchoative

We see that there is a Path-Place dynamics working in these examples, syntactically represented sometimes as {π, {P}} (Acedo Matellán & Mateu, 2010). More evident are the following examples, where the prepositional value is overt:

P: ex- (Latin / Spanish)
pro- (Latin)
ad- (Latin)
κατα- (Greek)
ανα- (Greek)
en/m- (Spanish)

The question is: why are they materialized "at the beginning" of the word (in purely linear terms)? One possible answer is that there is morphophonological movement *à la Nanosyntax* so as not to intervene in the local relation root-procedural head (D or T), taking as valid that the root is within the {P} structure, as depicted above, and thus closer to P than to D/T. This option banns spell-outs like:

(34)   *√red-*en-des-ar* (for *desenredar*, "untie")

As a descriptive generalization, this could very well work for the origin of prefixed words, but once the procedure has became fossilized, **creativity sticks to analogy, not to logic**. This is why we have apparent counter-examples, which are actually "modern" in their origin. Now, there is an essential question to be asked: *why would SM be sensitive to scope and local relations?* Two possible answers come to our mind:

- S-M has access to C-I
- S-M operates in an analogous way to C-I

The first option goes against the tenets of Massive Modularity, to which we stick for the moment (at least for the *interpretative systems*, see Kri-

---

thesis would be related to the fact that seeing an event in its development is, in locative terms, moving *towards* a location, but not yet being there.

vochen, 2011d), so that we will avoid that option if possible. The second, on the other hand, seems more plausible since, although it has been claimed that PF is the source of all variety and irregularity in language, the optimal scenario would be that in which *both C-I and S-M are ruled by third factor principles*. Claiming that SM is somehow different from C-I implies a stipulative distinction among interpretative systems which is taken for granted in Chomskyan work. So, morphophonological operations apply in S-M just as post-syntactic computations apply in C-I for explicature / implicature building (Wilson & Sperber, 2003, Krivochen, 2010a). The MFC is an S-M interface constraint on otherwise free Merge, as explicature building requirements are C-I interface constraints. Interfaces "peer into" syntax, and *Analyze* the output of every derivational step (Krivochen, 2011c). Merge, then, is free and unbounded in the working area, but the ill-formed products (in interface terms) are filtered out after transfer, if the violation could not be repaired in the next derivational step (see Putnam, 2010, for a soft version of "crash", related to this claim).

6 A note on compounds

Compounds, in our theory, are not formed in the syntax every time we have to use them if the word is already coined. That means that *coined compounds enter the derivation as a single root, rather than arising every time from the combination of two or more roots*. However, there is a time in which a compound is built (the "genesis" of the compound), and that is what we are going to analyze now.

There are two possibilities for representing the syntactic structure of a (yet) non-coined compound:

(35)

We will do away with the first one, since there is no procedural element to indicate the relation between both conceptual elements (i.e., roots). In the second representation we can see a null (or not) procedural node, which provides instructions to C-I as to how to manipulate the conceptual content conveyed by roots.

We propose the existence of two types of compounds:

a) Those compounds in which there is no "semantic requirement" involved (A-structural).

b) Those compounds in which there appears to be a "semantic requirement" involved.

Consequently, there are two main structures for compounds. We will analyze each in turn.

a) Azulgrana, albinegro/a, blanquiceleste, teórico-práctico/a, físico-químico/a.

b) Lavarropas, parabrisas, sacapuntas, secarropa, sacacorchos.

In the (a) group, we have two roots related by means of a procedural node, giving us a representation very much like those of De Belder (2011), but substituting the interface-dubious FP by a full procedural node that can be realized phonologically. The overall interpretation of the compound is that of a *noun* or an *adjective*, depending on the procedural head that is merged at the top, D or P respectively. Regardless categorial issues, what we have here is an *eventive unaccusative construal* (see Krivochen, 2011e). Let us take a look at the derivation:

(36)

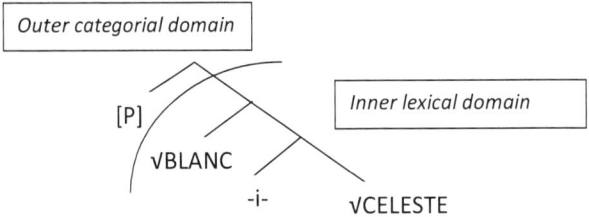

The introduction of the root √CELESTE in the workspace generates a non-legible object for the semantic interface, as roots are underspecified. However, as there is no transfer, no problem arises. The introduction of the procedural element [-*i*-] is very relevant at this respect, since it licenses the presence of a second conceptual element. Being a procedural linker by nature, this element is *relational*, and there must be something else to relate. The syntactic object in the inner lexical domain is a fully-fledged *relational* (ultimately, spatial) "projection" (taking into account that there are no heads or projections in our system), but it is not fully interpretable, as there is no procedural node that generates a *categorial interpretation*, which is necessary for explicature-building purposes. Therefore, the merger of a procedural node at the top is necessary, triggered by *Dynamic Full Interpretation* and following Putnam's (2010) *Soft Crash*. This procedural node would be the local derivational unit that fixes the violation in a syntactic object α, being α the inner domain.

Now, for labeling purposes, can Ø "project" (with all due comments about labeling and projection made)? If it is *radically empty*, as in De Belder's work, it cannot project. Two main reasons come to our mind:

a) If *Label* is seen as essentially *Copy*, then there is nothing to copy "upwards".
b) If *Label* is seen as an interface-driven recognition operation, then there would be nothing to recognize. The derivation would crash.

However, we have said that there are procedural dimensions in Ø, then those dimensions (basically, some instruction saying "there is a paratactic relation here") are recognized by the interface as the label, as if it were a {P} construction, with its (conceptual, not syntactic) *figure* and *ground*. It is time to ask ourselves: is this an optimal solution? No. Why? Because there is no reason to posit a label there anyway. In fact, things work better if *no label is posited*, and the structure remains active until either P or D are introduced in the working area, which are well-known categorial interpretation generators. This allows us to:

- Procrastinate C-I evaluation and *label* recognition.
- Procrastinate *Transfer*. In this way, we account for effects of *inner* and *outer* morphology without making reference to phase heads, but sticking to our non-stipulative system-neutral definition (Krivochen, 2010b, 2011a,):
  P is a phase in L_X iff it is the minimal term fully interpretable in L_{X+1}.

Now let us turn our attention to examples in group (b). Those examples are *caused compounds*, that is, there is a [Cause] primitive involved, and the resultant compounds are interpreted as if there was some semantic selection within. However, we have dispensed with features of all kinds, specially (categorial or semantic) selectional features. These imply a strong restriction for Merge, and we have made a case for *Free* Merge in our previous works. The structure we posit is the following:

(37)

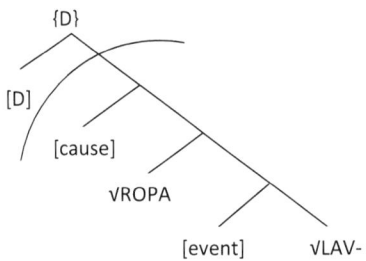

A question is in order here: do *caused* compounds license an external argument or initiator? That is, is the structure as we posit or actually [*pro* √lava-√ropas]? We believe not. Bear in mind that there is no [EPP] or any other requirement of the sort (Krivochen & Kosta, 2012), so there is no "*every clause must have a subject*" *a priori* constraint or requirement. As far as we are concerned, the interpretation of an external argument is purely inferential, as there is a {cause} node involved. This interpretation is a kind of "generic interpretation", of the type {UQ, √THING}, since it is impossible to restrict its reference (as there is no *Split T* above, see Krivochen, 2010a). This leads us to an interesting conclusion: *eventive compounds –in their syntactic structure, when it is modeled- are* **thetic**, that is, they have no *theme* (in informational terms). Remember that we have posited that the so-called "subject position" (i.e. Spec-TP) is a thematic position, and movement is semantically motivated, to interpret an element in that position as *theme* of the clause. *No external position means no theme* but perfectly possible parsing, which is a desirable result.

7 On coinage and derivation

Let us consider a derivation from the very beginning: the semantic-pragmatic "*global plan*" (Bernárdez, 1982). We assume, not innocently, that that intention is "embodied" in a RSS. Notice the fact that, if conceptual addresses can be freely combined in both Boeckx's and our model just because of their common format, there is nothing principled that can ban Merge of generic concepts, as they also share "format". This RSS is not manipulable by FL, as generic concepts are, as we have said here and in other works, not linguistic entities but *a-categorial* entities, severely *semantically underspecified*, and therefore, LF-defective (Panagiotidis,

2009, 2010). The information conveyed by the RSS must be carried along the derivation in order not to incur in a violation of the CP, and so generic concepts are instantiated as linguistically manipulable units, which we will refer to as *"roots"* (and that are equivalent to Boeckx's *conceptual addresses*). Now, we have linguistic entities, but *pre*-categorial linguistic entities, therefore, interface-defective. The difference with concepts in this respect is that concepts are *a*-categorial, that is, they cannot (basically, because they need not) bear a category. Category is not needed in the syntax (or at least not if we consider that Merge applies freely and syntax is blind), but it is needed in order to build an explicature in the post-syntactic instance of C-I. *Pre*-categoriality means that roots have the "inner potentiality" to be verbs or nouns. Can we say that certain roots are more likely to collapse to one state or the other? No, we cannot do so in a Radically Minimalist framework, as it would be an *unprincipled* statement. We must solve it otherwise. Let us consider the case of CAT. Is it possible to form a verbal morpheme (that is, a syntactic terminal node) to which a phonological piece /kæt/ corresponds? Yes, if the underlying construal has [CAT] (the generic concept) in a legitimate position. We cannot form a verb [$_V$ cat] from a semantic construal where CAT is on the external position licensed by the causative node, since we would be conflating the Spec into a Head, and such an operation would require many stipulations (and, in empirical terms, this would yield wrong interpretations, as Hale & Keyser, 1993 very well point out). This verb would be an *impossible word*[46]. If [CAT] appears within the locative node, for example, we could form a *locatum / location* verb [$_V$ cat] (for example, "to cat a mouse", meaning [CAUSE [GO [[mouse] [TO] [cat]]]] in Mateu's terms), and that would merely be a yet *uncoined word*, but perfectly *possible*, and *parseable* by the semantic component. The *Morpheme Formation Constraint* does not help when the morpheme has been formed according to "long-known principles of syntax" (think of GB's principles, for example). However, *rutinized neurological connections* do. Bear in mind that only *concatenation* comes "for free" (by conceptual necessity, in all physical sys-

---

46 The explanation for *impossible words* is very simple: Let us assume that we have [$_{XP}$ ZP [$_{X'}$ [X_0] YP]] and X_0 is defective, either phonologically or semantically. If we consider the diachronic dimension of the derivation, as soon as we have [X' [X_0] YP], following the *Earliness Principle*, the *conflation* process must occur. There is no need (and, what is more, it would be an anti-economical option) to wait until ZP is merged. *Dynamic Full Interpretation* also plays a role, as it triggers conflation to generate a fully interpretable object.

tems), the "lexicon" (by which we mean the *inventory of phonological pieces*, a purely socio-historical product), is *learned*. Learning is a process of adjustment of neurological connections, and when recurrent neurological flows (this time, to use a metaphor) are rutinized, the connection is made quicker, almost automatic (in a Fodorian way). There is evidence in favor of statistical learning within Generative Grammar (Thornton & Tesan, 2006, for example), and we could therefore experiment a bit with the idea.

Is it really the case that a root like √CAT is somehow more inclined to be merged with a D procedural node because of sme syntactic requirement or is it that, as the N is "more widely used" (because of sociohistorical factors, once again), and the phonological matrix is perceived in certain environments, the neurological connection is rutinized and the syntactic configuration reflects that statistical asymmetry by merging {D, √CAT} "by default", as the *most accessible (but not the only one) option for the inferential component to work with*?, thus following Relevance Principles. We think that assuming the first option would require special stipulations that would not be welcomed in our framework, (or in any form of minimalism, by the way). The problem must be analyzed, from our point of view, *the other way around*.

(38)

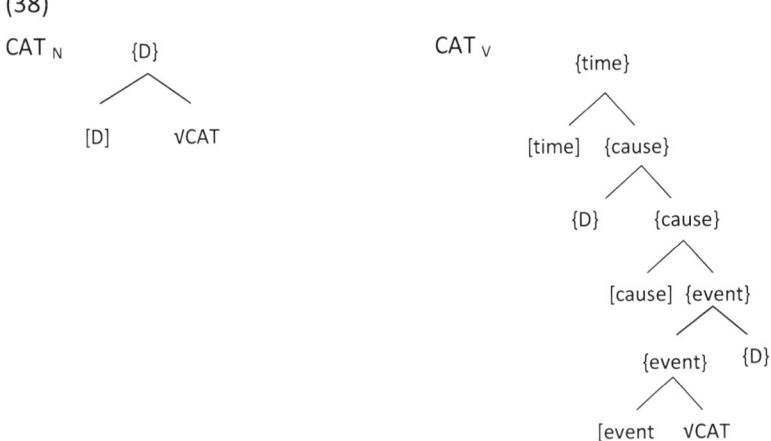

- The representations of locatum / location Vs differ in the RSS representation, but it is the same in the narrow syntax, as they are taken as fully-fledged *coined words*.

- The IA is licensed the relational node *r* in (di-)transitive construals. We have put it under the domain of [event], so that the conditions for dimension collapse obtain: *locality* and *c-command* (even though such a notion has little place in a strongly derivational model like ours). The "side" of the tree in which {D} appears is, of course, irrelevant[47].

There is, however, a problem that has been pointed out in previous literature on the topic: the possibility of so-called *"overgeneration"*. In order to address the issue, let us analyze the following examples, taken from Barner & Bale (2002) –the acceptability judgments are theirs-:

(39)
   a) ? John *spidered* yesterday.
   b) ? John *falled* in France this year.
   c) ? Don't *broom* my mess.
   d) ? I'm going to *basket* those apples.
   e) ? You're *gunning* him.
   f) ? He *Steve-ed* me again.

What they say at this respect is that:

> "(...) the sentences in (7) [our (39)] are not necessarily ungrammatical, but rather could be viewed as merely unacceptable. That is, the sentences do indeed sound bad, but not necessarily for reasons stemming from rules of grammar (indeed, no rule of grammar currently presents itself as a candidate for excluding these and allowing other flexible noun/verb uses). For example, the use of spider in example (7a) illustrates that certain forms may be suppressed due to a lack of cogent interpretation, largely stemming from a **lack of feasible pragmatic context** (Corbin, 1997; Dressler and Ladanyi, 2000; Marle, 1992). However, where context is sufficiently rich, such verb coinages become entirely acceptable, as is shown by (8) below.
>
> (8) The agile climber **spidered** up the face of the mountain." (p. 777. Our highlighting)

---

47 The reader may find similarities between our representation and Larson's (1988). However, he / she has surely became aware of the differences between both approaches. There are no heads in our model, no complements or adjuncts, as we are not working within an X-bar theoretical background. Another important note, which we will develop in future papers, is that syntax must work in 3-D, not in 2-D: trees are like atomic models, they help us visualize, but in no way are they accurate representations of structures built in the mind. The "side" of the tree branches appear in is now even more irrelevant.

Our analysis of Barner & Bale's claims will begin with the definition of the concept of *overgeneration*, a crucial concept for a *generative grammar* (Cf. Chapter 1)[48] and of particular importance for models of lexical generation:

(40) Given a generative system Σ, and a finite set $S = \{\alpha_1...\alpha_n\}$ of well-formed formulae, Σ generates both S **and** α_x, and $\alpha_x \notin S$.

Such concept needs S to be determined *beforehand*, that is, one builds a syntactic theory (an explanation of Σ) to account for a predetermined number of objects (S) arbitrarily selected, and there is no mention to *interface conditions* as regulators of syntactic activity. This position will be regarded as *strong constructivism* (see Lasnik, Uriagereka & Boeckx, 2005, for a case in favor of constructivism). RM, on the other hand, is a variant of *strong restrictivism*, a position that we already defined in Chapter 1 as follows:

(41) <u>Restrictivist theory:</u> *given a generative system Σ (Σ = Merge) and a set S of discrete units of whatever nature, Σ manipulates members of S freely and unboundedly, all constraints being determined by interface conditions.*

In a restrictivist theory no "well-formed" set is predefined, as there is no such thing as well-formedness in the syntax. Merge generates objects, which are in turn read by the interface levels, our focus being put on C-I.

The sentences in (38) are of course not "ungrammatical", as there is no such a concept in our model. Nor do we need any "pragmatic context" to interpret them, that is, to build an explicature. "*If we know the meaning, we know the structure, perforce, because we know the meaning from the structure*" (Hale & Keyser, 1997). Panagiotidis (2005) is right on pointing that we need something like Hale & Keyser's *conflation* process to account for verbs like those on (38), but, as we have said, those processes do not occur in the syntax, but roots are already *coined*, regardless whether coinage is *ad hoc* or it has a long history. Therefore, if we have:

(42) SPIDER $_V$

---

48 It is to be noticed that, from Chomsky (1965) on, the concept of *strong generation* (i.e., generation of structural descriptions) set the goal of syntactic theory within mainstream models: separate "grammatical" from "ungrammatical" and provide means to generate the whole set of grammatical strings, a position that we formalized in Chapter 1.

There are several possible interpretations, which will depend on the LF that reaches the interface:

a) *Unergative* V of manner of motion (John *spidered* up the wall: *Path of Motion* construction "he moved like a spider")
b) Transitive *locatum* V: this option needs a further inferential step, namely, an understanding of the metonymy involved in cases such as "John *spidered* Mary" when understood as "he trapped her like a spider would do". However, "John covered Mary with spiders" is the first parsing available and, therefore, the first one to be considered. If (and only if) that interpretation does not fulfill the Relevance expectations, the former option is computed.

Contrarily to our free-generation system, Panagiotidis (2005: 1188) points out that:

> "(...) there is a number of nouns that seem to avail themselves of no corresponding verb, no matter how we stretch our capability for coining; some examples include: *poem, dialogue, sonnet, limerick, alexandrine*. What we would be forced to say of the corresponding roots is that something blocks the relevant syntactic process and they cannot be inserted in CPs to become verbs." (our highlighting)

On the *empirical* side, we disagree with Panagiotidis on the following: there is no such a thing as "capability for coining". There is a phonological matrix that is inserted on a terminal root node, if that root (with additional material, if necessary) appears in the local domain of T, it will be *interpreted* as V, whereas if it is within the domain of D, it will be *interpreted* as N. Besides, in a free Merge system, with no constraints as to where roots can appear, every root has equal possibility of surfacing as V or N, regardless of the fact that it has been attested or not. Let us analyse an example:

(42) John *poemed / sonneted* Mary (locatum V)

That is a yet *"uncoined"* expression (to our knowledge), but it could very well be generated and it is perfectly interpretable *at both interfaces*. The derivational path, from the very beginning, would be the following:

(43)
Relational Semantic Structure (C-l₁):   Syntactic instantiation:

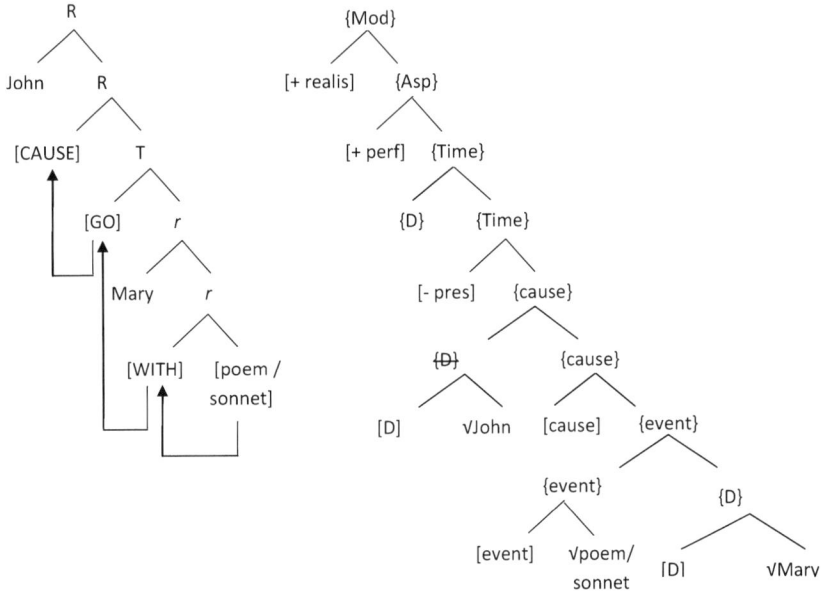

(44)
Lower-level explicature (C-l₂):
- Decoding: recover the subjacent semantic structure (RSS), interpret who the participants are and what role they play in the event (*interpretation of A-structure and theta-roles*, Krivochen, 2010c). The interpretation of "what [to poem /sonnet] means" occurs at this point, using the clues given by the syntactic structure.
- Disambiguation: there are no ambiguous expressions in this particular example (but see Sperber & Wilson, 2003 for an account of "bank" as an ambiguous expression).
- Referent assignment: (see Krivochen 2010a for extended discussion and data analysis in Spanish) procedural features of D enter into play. Proper names are usually interpreted as definite, but with common names the interpretation depends on the local relation of {D} and features of Time, Aspect and Modality.

- <u>Semantic enrichment</u>: not determined by any element present in the syntax or LF (who John is, why would he want to "sonnet" Mary, etc.).

Possibilities depend on the semantic properties of the root: √BOTTLE, for example, allows the location / locatum alternation, but the unergative option is hardly relevant (but not entirely clashing), therefore, it is not likely to be considered when building an explicature. *"X's unpredictability" is just "(our) not being used to X as the most relevant interpretation"*, assuming that the first option is the most systematic one. Therefore, we conclude that there are no **ungrammatical** options, just **irrelevant** options.

On the *theoretical* side, our objection is related to how to encode the apparent asymmetry Panagiotidis points out. Needless to say, there is no need for positing such asymmetry in our system, and that is an important point in favor of our model, as the asymmetry is ultimately an additional stipulation.

To summarize this section, *coinage* is taken as a process of neurological rutinization. Even if we accept *lexical decomposition* models as explanations of the essentially syntactic nature of lexical derivations and, in fact, the rejection of the theoretical weight of the s-syntax / l-syntax distinction, it is unrealistic and implausible, given the fact that our working capacity is limited, to think that derivations actually proceed from the nano-syntactic level to a fully fledged phrasal construction in real time. It is simply not necessary to derive a construal and then look for the Vocabulary Item (VI) that best Spells-Out the dimensions present in the relevant construal if the construal is already stored in the Long Time Memory (LTM) as an atomic unit and the link to the VI (possibly, neurologically stored in Brocca's area) is already "fixed" due to frequent access. We therefore limit the range of action of lexical decomposition models which, even though strongly explanatory and predictive, cannot be used for the derivation of a sentence with coined words when access to LTM and storage of structures as atomic units in a W_X is a simpler option. This is a point in favor of Uriagareka's (1998) thesis that lexical derivations are not productive, or systematic, or transparent. However, admitting such a theory to have universal validity would imply neglecting the generative capacity that allows natural languages to create new words (both structures and VIs) or use known words in different environments (like "to *poem* somebody"), which is too common a practice to dismiss it. Consequently, we restrict the applicability of lexical decomposition models (e.g.,

Hale & Keyser, 1993, 2002, to some extent, Halle & Marantz, 1993, Embick & Noyer, 2004) to *possible* words, whereas the interaction between Brocca's area and LTM (where structures are stored), can be used in a sketch of a theory of lexical knowledge (which exceeds by far the limits of the present monograph).

8 Conclusion

In this chapter we have put RM to test with problematic phenomena in languages from different families (Germanic, Slavic and Romance), circumscribing ourselves to the nominal domain, but occasionally making broader considerations on lexical syntax and semantics. The choice of languages was not random: we have seen that RM can account for interlinguistic variation without resorting to special stipulations of dubious biological plausibility. Notice that we have used nothing more than the initial set of procedural elements (P, D, Tense, Cause, Event, with the addition of so-called Top when we had to account for drastic interface effects) and semantically underspecified roots, and a single free generative algorithm, constrained by two interface principles (DFI and CP). The empirical advantages of RM over traditional and orthodox generative accounts are at this point clear, which does not mean that they are free from criticism. Nevertheless, the degree of methodological and substantive simplicity RM has achieved without losing empirical coverage is hardly arguable, as this chapter has shown. We encourage the interested reader to apply RM to problematic structures in his/her own language, and put the theory to test.

Chapter 4: Conclusion

In this work we have presented a newly developed framework: Radical Minimalism. It has characteristics that define it more as a *program* than as a *theory*, since it actually consists on very basic substantive claims summarized in the SRMT and has far reaching consequences for many fields, like mathematics, physics, biology and, of course, linguistics. Perhaps the greatest contribution RM can make is precisely the initiative to tear the walls between these fields down: if Tegmark's hypothesis that the physical reality is a mathematical structure, then the highest aim of scientific inquiry is to make this mathematical structure explicit in unambiguous terms. The present monograph, however, has a much narrower scope, yet not any less important: we have tested the explanatory and descriptive adequacy of the theorems derivable from the theory in the domain of Nominal Constructions (NC). To this end, we took a "general-to-particular" path: we first described the framework with special reference to the consequences its adoption yields for linguistics, making occasional comparisons with other alternative frameworks to orthodox mainstream Minimalism, like Survive Minimalism and Optimality Theory. From those comparisons, RM emerged as a viable alternative, particularly given its strong mathematical roots, which allow unambiguous formalization, and versatility.

In more specific terms, RM explores a long-ignored interface, particularly from Generative perspectives (even though semanticists have neglected syntax just as much): syntax-semantics. The usual path to take in descriptive grammar, which was perhaps unconsciously maintained in Generative Grammar (as well as Systemic Functional Linguistics and Text Grammar), was "from phonology to syntax". This is, given a certain string of phonological exponents, chunks of sounds are identified with syntactic units, say, constituents. The description of the function of these constituents was, and still is to a great extent, made in function of their place in the phonological string. This methodology implies a close relation between syntax and phonology, while wiping semantics under the rug. This relation reached its maximum exponent with Kayne's (1994) LCA, and subsequent work. In RM the opposite alternative is pursued: syntactic structure must be a function of semantics, since it is the semantic component that defines language as such: phonology is merely a means of externalization, parasitic to language in its strictest sense: a generative component, which we have formalized as the operation *concatenation* and an interpretative component that drives the generation and guarantees a *crash-proof* derivation by means of *Dynamic Full Interpretation*. Notice that the principles we manage are, crucially, not exclusive of linguistic description, but can be applied in any derivation independently of the units that are manipulated and the physical substratum that licenses the computational properties of the system. Our principles stem from mathematical research, and, as such, are not constrained by biological considerations. If the physical reality is indeed a mathematical structure, then physics as a whole is a subset of possible physics that describe the behavior of theoretical Universes. Within such a framework (the norm in current theoretical physics), biology is a particular instantiation of possible physical configurations. Should we depart from biology, a deeper understanding of the ruling principles of the physical reality will very hardly be gained. However, the inverse path seems very promising, and is the path Radical Minimalism has taken.

This work has been concerned with the derivation and interpretation of NC, but the reader should bear in mind that the potential and scope of RM are that of a *program*, not a *theory*. Whether we are on the right track, only time can tell.

Bibliography

Abels, K. (2003) Successive Cyclicity, Anti-locality and Adposition Stranding. Ph.D. Thesis. University of Connecticut, Storrs.
Abney, S.P. (1987) The English Noun Phrase in its Sentential Aspect. PhD Thesis, MIT.
Acedo-Matellán, Víctor & Jaume Mateu (2010) *From satellite-framed Latin to verb-framed Romance: A syntactic approach.* Universitat Autónoma de Barcelona. Departament de Filología Catalana. http://filcat.uab.cat/clt/membres/professors/mateu.html
Adger, D. (2008) *A Minimalist Theory of Feature Structure.* lingBuzz/000583(2011) *Labels and Structures.* lingBuzz /001252
Adger, D. & P. Sevenoius (2010) *Features in Minimalist Syntax.* lingBuzz/000825
Alexiadou, A. (2003) *Functional Structure in Nominals: Nominalization and Ergativity.* Linguistics Today 42. Amsterdam, John Benjamins.
Alexiadou, A., M. Stavrou and L. Haegeman (2007), *Noun Phrase in the Generative Perspective.* Berlin/New York: Mouton de Gruyter.
Alexopoulou, T. & F. Keller (2003) Linguistic Complexity, Locality and Resumption. In *WCCFL 22 Proceedings*, ed. G. Garding and M. Tsujimura. Somerville, MA: Cascadilla Press.

Barner, D. & A. Bale (2002) *No Nouns, no Verbs: Psycholinguistic Arguments in Favor of Lexical Underspecification.* In "Lingua" 112, 771-791.
Barner, D. & A. Bale (2005) *No Nouns, no Verbs? A Rejoinder to Panagiotidis.* In "Lingua" 115, 1169-1179.
Bernárdez, E. (1982) "Introducción a la Lingüística del Texto". Madrid, Epasa.
Boeckx, C. (2008) Treelets, not Trees. *BCGL 3 — Trees and Beyond.* May 21–23, 2008
Boeckx, C. (2009) "The Nature of Merge. Consequences for Language, Mind and Biology". In Piatelli Palmarini et. al. *Of Minds and Language.* Oxford, OUP.
Boeckx, C. (2010) *Defeating Lexicocentrism.* lingBuzz/001130
Boeckx, C. & K.K. Grohmann (2007) "Putting phases in perspective". In *Syntax* 10: 204-222.
Bosque, I. y Gutiérrez Rexach, J. (2008) *Fundamentos de sintaxis formal* Madrid, Akal.

Borer, H. (2009) Roots and Categories. Handout presented at *XIX Colloquium on Generative Grammar*, University of the Basque Country.

Carruthers, P. (2006). *The Architecture of the Mind*. Oxford: Oxford University Press.

Carston, R. (1998) *The Relationship between Generative Grammar and (Relevance-theoretic) Pragmatics*. University College, London.

Chomsky, N. (1957) *Syntactic Structures*. Mouton, The Hague.

Chomsky, N. (1965) *Aspects of the Theory of Syntax*. Cambridge, Mass. MIT Press.

Chomsky, N. (1970) Remarks on Nominalization. In Chomsky, N. (1972) *Studies in Semantics in Generative Grammar*. Mouton, The Hague.

Chomsky, N. (1981) *Lectures on Government and Binding*, Dordrecht, Foris.

Chomsky, N. (1982) *Some Concepts and Consequences of the Theory of Government and Binding*. LI Monographs 6. MIT Press.

Chomsky, N. (1986) *Barriers*. MIT LI Monographs 13. Cambridge, Mass. MIT press.

Chomsky, N. (1994) Bare Phrase Structure. *MIT Occasional Papers in Linguistics 5*. MIT Press.

Chomsky, N. (1995) *The Minimalist Program*. Cambridge, Mass. MIT press.

Chomsky, N. (1998) Minimalist Inquiries: The Framework. *MIT Occasional Papers in Linguistics 15*.

Chomsky, N. (1999) Derivation by Phase. *MIT Occasional Papers in Linguistics 18*.

Chomsky, N. (2004) Beyond Explanatory Adequacy. In Belleti (ed.) *Structures and Beyond*, 104-131. Oxford, OUP.

Chomsky, N. (2005a) On Phases. Ms. MIT.

Chomsky, N. (2005b) Three Factors in Language Design. *Linguistic Inquiry Vol. 36 n° 1*, 1-22- MIT press.

Chomsky, N. (2007) Approaching UG from below. Ms. MIT.

Chomsky, N. (2009) Opening Remarks. In Piatelli Palmarini et. al. *Of Minds and Language*. Oxford, OUP.

Cinque, G. (1999) *Adverbs and Functional Heads. A Cross-linguistic Perspective*, New York, Oxford University Press.

Collins, C. (2002) Eliminating Labels. In *Derivation and Explanation in the Minimalist Program*, ed. S.D. Epstein & T.D. Seely, pp. 42-64. Oxford: Blackwell.

De Belder, M. (2011) Roots and Affixes: Eliminating Categories from Syntax. PhD Thesis, Utrecht University.
De Belder, M. & J. Van Craenenbroeck (2011) How to Merge a Root. LingBuzz 001226.
Dehaene, S. (2011) *Space, Time and Number in the Brain: Searching for the Foundations of Mathematical Thought*. Academic Press.
De Lancey, S. (2001) *Lectures on Functional Syntax.* University of Oregon.
Di Sciullo, A-M. & C. Boeckx (eds.) (2011) *The Biolinguistic Enterprise: New Perspectives on the Evolution and Nature of the Human Language Faculty*. Oxford, OUP.
Di Sciullo, A-M. & D. Isac, (2008) The Asymmetry of Merge. In *Biolinguistics 2.4*: 260–290
Dowty, D. (1991) Thematic Proto-roles and Argument Selection, *Language* 67 (3): 547-619

Eguren, L. (1993) "Núcleos de Frase". In *Verba*, 20, pp. 61-91.
Einstein, A. (1905) On the Electrodynamics of Moving Bodies. *In* Annalen der Physik *(ser. 4)*, **17**, 891–921
Embick, D. (2010) *Localism versus Globalism in Morphology and Phonology*. Cambridge, Mass. MIT Press.
Embick, D. & R. Noyer (2004) Distributed Morphology and the Syntax-Morphology Interface. Draft: 25/10/2004
Epstein, S. (1999) Un-Principled Syntax and the Derivation of Syntactic Relations. In *Working Minimalism*, S. Epstein, and N. Hornstein, eds. MIT Press, Cambridge, MA.
Epstein, S. & T. Seely (2000) SPEC-ifying the GF Subject: Eliminating A-Chains and the EPP within a Derivational Model. Ms. University of Michigan.
Epstein, S. & T. Seely (2002) Rule Applications as Cycles in a Level Free Syntax. In *Derivation and Explanation in the Minimalist Program*, ed. S.D. Epstein & T.D. Seely, 65-89. Oxford: Blackwell.
Epstein, S. & T. Seely (2006) *Derivations in Minimalism*. Cambridge, CUP.
Escandell Vidal, M.V. (2006) *Introducción a la Pragmática*. Barcelona, Ariel.
Escandell Vidal, M.V. & M. Leonetti (2000), Categorías conceptuales y semántica procedimental. In *Cien años de investigación semántica: de Michél Bréal a la actualidad. Tomo I*, Madrid, Ediciones clásicas, 363-378.
Escandel Vidal, M. V., M. Leonetti & A. Ahern (eds.), (2011) *Procedural Meaning*. Bingley: Emerald (Crispi Series)

Evans, G. (1982) *The Varieties of Reference*. Oxford, OUP.

Fábregas, A. (2005) La definición de la categoría gramatical en una morfología orientada sintácticamente: nombres y adjetivos. PhD Thesis, Universidad Autónoma de Madrid.

Fábregas, A. (2010) An Argument for Phasal Spell-Out. *Nordlyd 36, Special Issue on Nanosyntax*, ed. Peter Svenonius, Gillian Ramchand, Michal Starke, and Tarald Taraldsen, CASTL, Tromsø.

Gallego, A. (2007) Phase Theory and Parametric Variation. PhD Thesis, Universitat Autónoma de Barcelona.

Gallego, A. (2010) *Phase Theory*. Amsterdam, John Benjamins.

Gazdar, G. (1979) *Pragmatics: Implicature, Presupposition, and Logical Form*. New York: Academic.

Grohmann, K. K. (2003) *Prolific Domains. On the Anti-Locality of Movement Dependencies*. Amsterdam: John Benjamins.

Grohmann, K. K. (2004) Prolific Domains in the Computational System. In *Actas de JEL 2004: Domains*. Nantes: AAI, 211-216.

Haegeman, L. & J. Gueron (1999) *English Grammar: A Generative Perspective*. Oxford, Blackwell.

Hale, K. & J. Keyser (1993) On Argument Structure and the Lexical Expression of Syntactic Relations. In Hale & Keyser (1993) *The View from Building 20*, 53-110. Cambridge, Mass. MIT Press.

Hale, K. & J. Keyser (1997a) On the Complex Nature of Simple Predicators. In A. Alsina, J. Bresnan & P. Sells (eds.), *Complex Predicates*, pp. 29-65. Stanford: CSLI Publications.

Hale, K. & J. Keyser (1997b) *The Basic Elements of Argument Structure*. Ms. MIT.

Hale, K. & J. Keyser (2002) *Conflation*. Ms. MIT.

Halle, M. & A. Marantz (1993) Distributed Morphology and the Pieces of Inflection. In Hale & Keyser (eds.). 111-176.

Heisenberg, W. (1999) *Physics and Philosophy*, New York: Prometheus Books

Hendrick, R. (2003) *Minimalist Syntax*. Oxford, Blackwell.

Hinzen, W. (2009) Hierarchy, Merge and Truth. In Piatelli Palmarini et. al. *Of Minds and Language*. Oxford, OUP.

Jackendoff, R. (1977) *X-bar Syntax: a Study of Phrase Structure.* Linguistic Inquiry Monographs 2. MIT Press.

Jackendoff, R. (2002) *Fundamentos del lenguaje*. México, FCE.

Kager, R. (1999) *Optimality Theory*. Cambridge University Press, Cambridge.
Kayne, R. (1994) *The Antisymmetry of Syntax*. Cambridge, Mass. MIT Press.
Kosta, P. (2003): Negation and Adverbs in Czech, in: Kosta, P., Błaszczak, J., Frasek, J., Geist, L. & M. Żygis (eds.) *Investigations into Formal Slavic Linguistics: Proceedings of the Fourth European Conference on Formal Description of Slavic Languages - FDSL 4, Potsdam, 28-30 November 2001.* (Linguistik International 10.1-2). (Frankfurt am Main, Berlin, Bern, Bruxelles, New York, Oxford, Wien: Peter Lang, 2003), S. 601-616.
Kosta, P. (2006) On free word order phenomena in Czech as compared to German: Is Clause Internal Scrambling A-movement, A-Bar-Movement or Is It Base Generated? In: *Zeitschrift für Slawistik 51 (2006) 3, S. 306-321.*
Kosta, P. (2008) Quantification of NPs/DPs in Slavic. In: Peter Kosta / Daniel Weiss (Hrsg.). *Slavistische Linguistik 2006/2007. Beiträge zum XXXII. / XXXIII.* Konstanzer Slavistischen Arbeitstreffen in Boldern und Potsdam (03.09.-06.09.2007). München: Sagner 2008, 247-266
Kosta, P. (2009) Targets, Theory and Methods of Slavic Generative Syntax: Minimalism, Negation and Clitics. In *Slavic Languages: An International Handbook of their Structure, their History and their Investigation.* Herausgegeben von / Edited by Sebastian Kempgen, Peter Kosta, Tilman Berger, Karl Gutschmidt. Band 1 / Volume 1. Walter de Gruyter · Berlin · New York. 282-316.
Kosta, P. (2010) Causatives and Anti-Causatives, Unaccusatives and Unergatives: Or How Big is the Contribution of the Lexicon to Syntax, in: Aleš Bican et al. (eds.), *Karlík a továrna na lingvistiku Prof. Petru Karlíkovi k šedesátým narozeninám,* Brno 2010, 230-273.
Kosta, P. & A. Zimmerling (2011) Slavic systems with Clitics and Syntactic typology. In: L. Schürcks, A. Giannakidou, U. Etxteberria and P. Kosta (eds.): *The Structure of NP and Beyond*, Berlin, New York: de Gruyter (Studies in Generative Grammar).
Koster, J. 2010. *Language and tools.* Ms., Universiteit Groningen
Krivochen, D. (2010a) Referencialidad y Definitud en D. Un análisis desde la convergencia entre el Programa Minimalista y la Teoría de la Relevancia. UNLP / Universidad Nacional de Rosario.
Krivochen, D. (2010b) Algunas notas sobre fases. UNLP. Presented at the conference "I Jornadas de Jóvenes Lingüistas", UBA, March, 2011.

Krivochen, D. (2010c) θ-Theory Revisited. UNLP. LingBuzz 001240.

Krivochen, D. (2010d) Prolegómenos a una teoría de la mente. UNLP. Unpublished.

Krivochen, D. (2011a) On the Syntax of Raising Verbs. UNLP. lingBuzz/001172.

Krivochen, D. (2011b) An Introduction to Radical Minimalism I: on Merge and Agree (and related issues). In *IBERIA Vol 3 n° 2*. Pp. 20-62.

Krivochen, D. (2011c) An Introduction to Radical Minimalism II: Internal Merge Beyond Explanatory Adequacy. lingBuzz/001256

Krivochen, D. (2011d) Unified Syntax. Ms. UNLP lingBuzz/001298

Krivochen, D. (2011e) The Quantum Human Computer Hypothesis and Radical Minimalism: A Brief Introduction to Quantum Linguistics. Published in *International Journal of Linguistic Studies* Vol. 5 n° 4, pp. 87-108.

Krivochen, D. (2011f) The Syntax of Spanish Relational Adjectives. Published in *Sorda y Sonora* (PUCP) vol. 2, n° 1.

Krivochen, D. (2012a) Towards a Geometrical Syntax. Ms. Universität Potsdam.

Krivochen, D. (2012b) Prospects for a Radically Minimalist OT. Ms. Universität Potsdam.

Krivochen, D. & P. Kosta (2011) Some (Radically Mimimalist) Thoughts on Merge. Presented at the Conference *Minimalist Program, Quo Vadis?* October 3-6, Potsdam University.

Krivochen, D. & P. Kosta (in press) *Eliminating Empty Categories*. Ms. Universität Potsdam. To appear in LFAB (John Benjamins Publishing Company).

Lakatos, I. (1978) *The Methodology of Scientific Research Programmes: Philosophical Papers Volume 1*. Cambridge: Cambridge University Press

Lasnik, H; J. Uriagereka & C. Boeckx (2005) *A Course in Minimalist Syntax*. Oxford, Blackwell.

Leonetti, M. (1996) *El artículo definido y la construcción del contexto*. En Revista Signo y Seña número 5, Febrero de 1996, FFyL, UBA.

Leonetti, M. (1999) *El artículo*. En Bosque y Demonte (eds.) Gramática Descriptiva de la Lengua Española. Real Academia Española, Colección Nebrija y Bello, Espasa, 1999. Volumen 1.

Leonetti, M. (2000) *The Asymmetries Between the Definite Article and Demonstratives: a Procedural Account*. Comunicación en la *VII International Pragmatics Conference*, Budapest. Inédito.

Leonetti, M. (2004) *Sobre tiempos y determinantes*. Actas del V Congreso de Lingüística General, Madrid, Arco, 2004.

Marantz, A. (1997) No Escape from Syntax: Don't Try Morphological Analysis in the Privacy of Your Own Lexicon. En A. Dimitriadis, L. Siegel, C. Surek-Clark, and A. Williams, eds., *Proceedings of the 21st Penn Linguistics Colloquium*, UPenn Working Papers in Linguistics, Philadelphia.

Mateu Fontanals, J. (2000a) Universals of Semantic Construal for Lexical Syntactic Relations. Ms. Universitat Autónoma de Barcelona. Departament de Filología Catalana.

Mateu Fontanals, J. (2000b) Why Can't We Wipe the Slate Clean?. Universitat Autónoma de Barcelona. Departament de Filología Catalana.

Martin, R. & J. Uriagereka (2011) On the Nature of Chains in Minimalism. Talk delivered at the conference *Minimalist Program: Quo Vadis?* Universität Potsdam, October 3-6, 2011.

Miechowickz-Mathiasen, K. (2009) There is no independent EPP in Slavic, there are only EPP-effects In: Zybatow, G., D. Lenertova, U. Junghanns, and P. Biskup (eds.) *Studies in Formal Slavic Phonology, Morphology, Syntax, Semantics and Information Structure: Proceedings of FDSL-7*, Leipzig 2007. Frankfurt am Main: Peter Lang.

Miechowickz-Mathiasen, K. (2011a) On the distribution and D-like properties of the Polish pronominal adjective "sam". Talk delivered at *Workshop on Languages with and without articles*, Paris, March 3rd 2011.

Miechowickz-Mathiasen, K. (2011b) Case, Tense and Clausal Arguments in Polish. Ms. Adam Mickiewicz University, Poland.

Miechowickz-Mathiasen, K. (2011c) Licensing Polish Higher Numerals: an Account of the Accusative Hypothesis. To appear in: *Generative Linguistics in Wrocław*, Vol. 2.

Miechowicz-Mathiasen, K. & D. Krivochen (in preparation) *Numerals and Cognition: Radical Minimalism and the Localist Theory*. Ms. Adam Mickiewicz University & Universität Potsdam.

Müller, G. (2011a) *Constraints on Displacement: a Phase-Based Approach*. Amsterdam, John Benjamins.

Müller, G. (2011b) *Optimality Theoretic Syntax*. Ms. Universität Leipzig. http://www.uni-leipzig.de/~muellerg/

Nunes, J. (2004) *Linearization of Chains and Sidewards Movement*. Linguistic Inquiry Monographs 43. MIT Press.

Panagiotidis, P. (2002) *Pronouns, clitics and empty nouns*. (Linguistik Aktuell 46). Amsterdam & Philadelphia: John Benjamins.
Panagiotidis, P. (2005) Against category-less roots in syntax and word learning: objections to Barner and Bale (2002). In *Lingua* 115, 1181–1194.
Panagiotidis, P. (2010) *Categorial Features and Categorizers*. Ms. University of Cyprus.
Pesetsky, D. and E. Torrego (2000) T-to-C movement: Causes and consequences. In: Kenstowicz, K. (ed.), *Ken Hale: A Life in Language*. Cambridge, MA: MIT Press.
Pesetsky, D. and E. Torrego (2004) The Syntax of Valuation and the Interpretability of Features. Ms. MIT / UMass Boston.
Pesetsky, D. and E. Torrego (2007) Probes, Goals and Syntactic Categories. In *Proceedings of the 7th annual Tokyo Conference on Psycholinguistics* (Keio University, Japan)
Prince, A. & P. Smolensky (2004): *Optimality Theory. Constraint Interaction in Generative Grammar*. Blackwell, Oxford.
Putnam, M. (Ed.) (2010) *Exploring Crash-Proof Grammars*. LFAB Series, edited by Pierre Pica & Kleanthes K. Grohmann. Amsterdam, John Benjamins.
Putnam, M. & T. Stroik (2011) Syntax at Ground Zero. Ms. Penn State University. To appear in *Linguistic Analysis*.

Quine, W. (1960) *Word and Object*. Cambridge, Mass. CUP.

Radeva-Bork, T. (2012), *Single and Double Cliticization in Bulgarian*, PhD diss. University of Vienna
Rizzi, L. (1990) *Relativized Minimality*. Cambridge, Mass. MIT Press
Rizzi, L. (1997) The Fine Structure of the Left Periphery. In Haegeman, L. (ed.) *Elements of Grammar*, 281-337. Dodrecht, Kluwer.
Rizzi, L. (2004) Locality and Left Periphery, in A. Belletti, ed., *Structures and Beyond – The Cartography of Syntactic Structures, Vol 3*, 223-251. Oxford University Press.
Russell, B. (1905) *On Denoting. Mind*, New Series, Vol. 14, No. 56. (Oct., 1905), pp. 479-493.

Schrödinger, E. (1935) The Present Situation in Quantum Mechanics. in *Proceedings of the American Philosophical Society*, 124. 323-338.
Smolensky, P & G. Legendre (2006) *The Harmonic Mind*. Mass. MIT Press.
Sperber, D. (2005) Modularity and relevance: How can a massively modular mind be flexible and context-sensitive? In *The Innate Mind:*

Structure and Content. Edited by Peter Carruthers, Stephen Laurence & Stephen Stich.

Sperber, D. y D. Wilson (1986a) Sobre la definición de Relevancia. En Valdés Villanueva, Luis Ml. (Comp.) (1991) *En búsqueda del significado*. 583-598. Madrid, Tecnos.

Sperber, D. y D. Wilson (1986b/1995) *Relevance: Communication and Cognition*. Oxford. Blackwell.

Strawson, P. (1950) On Referring. In *Mind* 59, pp. 320-344

Stroik, T & M. Putnam (in press) *The Structural Design of Language*. To appear in CUP.

Talmy, L. (2000) *Toward a Cognitive Semantics.* Cambridge, MA: Massachusetts Institute of Technology.

Tegmark, M. (2003) Parallel Universes. In *Scientific American Magazine* pp. 41-51. May, 2003.

Tegmark, M. (2007) The Mathematical Universe Hypothesis. In *Foundations of Physics*, 2007. http://arxiv.org/pdf/0704.0646v2.pdf

Ticio, M. E. (2010) *Locality Domains in the Spanish Determiner Phrase*. Studies in Natural Language and Linguistic Theory 79, Springer.

Uriagereka, J. (1998) *Pies y Cabeza*. Madrid, Visor.

Uriagereka, J. (1999) Multiple Spell-Out. In N. Hornstein & S. Epstein (eds.), *Working Minimalism*, Cambdridge (Mass.), MIT Press, 251-282.

Uriagereka, J. (2002) Multiple Spell-Out. In Uriagereka, J. *Derivations: Exploring the Dynamics of Syntax*, 45-66. London, Routledge.

Wurmbrand, S. (2011) Reverse Agree. Ms. University of Connecticut.

Yus, F. (2010) Relevance Theory. In: *The Oxford Handbook of Linguistic Analysis*. Eds. B. Heine and H. Narrog. Oxford: Oxford University Press, 679-701.

Potsdam Linguistic Investigations
Potsdamer Linguistische Untersuchungen
Recherches Linguistique à Potsdam

Edited by / Herausgegeben von / Edité par
Peter Kosta, Gerda Haßler, Teodora Radeva-Bork,
Lilia Schürcks and / und / et Nadine Thielemann

Band 1   Peter Kosta / Lilia Schürcks (eds.): Linguistics Investigations into Formal Description of Slavic Languages. Contributions of the Sixth European Conference held at Potsdam University, November 30–December 02, 2005. 2007.

Band 2   Lilia Schürcks: Binding and Discourse. Where Syntax and Pragmatics Meet. 2008.

Band 3   Christiane Hümmer: Synonymie bei phraseologischen Einheiten. Eine korpusbasierte Untersuchung. 2009.

Band 4   Svetlana Friedrich: Definitheit im Russischen. 2009.

Band 5   Matthias Guttke: Strategien der Persuasion in der schriftkonstituierten politischen Kommunikation. Dargestellt an Parteiprogrammen der Neuen Rechten in Polen. 2010.

Band 6   Peter Kosta / Lilia Schürcks (eds.): Formalization of Grammar in Slavic Languages. Contributions of the Eighth International Conference on Formal Description of Slavic Languages – FDSL VIII 2009. University of Potsdam, December 2–5, 2009. 2011.

Band 7   Roman Sukač (ed.): From Present to Past and Back. Papers on Baltic and Slavic Accentology. 2011.

Band 8   Diego Gabriel Krivochen: The Syntax and Semantics of Nominal Construction. A Radically Minimalist Perspective. 2012.

www.peterlang.de